William Lee Golden

Barbara Mandrell

Ronnie Milsap

Bobby Bare

Tanya Tucker

Dolly

Tammy Wynette

Mel Tillis

Jerry Reed

B.J. Thomas

Ricky Skaggs

Naomi Ellen Judd

Brenda Lee

Minnie Pearl

COOKING

WITH

COUNTRY MUSIC Stars

PELICAN PUBLISHING COMPANY

Gretna 1990

First printing, October 1986
Second printing, June 1987
First Pelican printing, April 1990

Library of Congress Cataloging-in-Publication Data

Cooking with country music stars.
       p. cm.
    ISBN 0-88289-793-4
    1. Cookery. 2. Country musicians--United States--
    Miscellanea.
    TX714.C657 1990   89-49642
    641-5--dc20   CIP

The recipes in this cookbook have been submitted by country music stars and have been edited for consistency. The publishers and editors accept no responsibility for recipes that seem to be unsatisfactory.

Manufactured in Hong Kong
Published by Pelican Publishing Company, Inc.
1101 Monroe Street, Gretna, Louisiana 70053

Stars

Alabama's Mark Herndon 10
Deborah Allen 12
Bill Anderson 14
Bobby Bare 16
Earl Thomas Conley 18
Helen Cornelius 20
Charlie Daniels 22
Little Jimmy Dickens 38
Lee Greenwood 40
Tom T. Hall 42
Emmylou Harris 44
The Judds 46
Pee Wee King 48
Brenda Lee 50
Barbara Mandrell 82
Reba McEntire 84
Ronnie Milsap 86
Michael Martin Murphey 88
The Oak Ridge Boys 90
Dolly Parton 92
Minnie Pearl 94
Eddy Raven 140
Jerry Reed 142
Kenny Rogers 144
T.G. Sheppard 146
Ricky Skaggs 148
The Statler Brothers 150
Ray Stevens 152
George Strait 154
B.J. Thomas 192
Mel Tillis 194
Tanya Tucker 196
Conway Twitty 198
Kitty Wells 200
The Whites 202
Hank Williams Jr. 204
Tammy Wynette 206

Table
of Contents

Foreword 6

Introduction 8

Soups and Salads 24

Veggies, Breads and Extras 52

Main Dishes 96

Desserts and Drinks 156

Index by Stars 208

Index by Recipe 212

Foreword

A wise man once said: "Kissing don't last; cooking do." He had a point there. Nothing sticks with you like good cooking.

The recipes in this book are all favorites of country music's biggest stars (and country music's top cooks!). Their recipes and their life stories appear here through the efforts of the staff here at the Country Music Foundation.

The Foundation is the largest and most active popular music research center in the world. Located in the heart of Nashville's historic Music Row, the Foundation has gained international recognition for its Country Music Hall of Fame and Museum, as well as for its massive library of recordings, books, periodicals, and songbooks available to journalists and researchers.

The Foundation's wide-ranging activities also encompass an oral history project, a reissue record label, educational outreach programs, the operation

of a recording studio as a historic site and learning lab, consultation services, a museum store and mail-order service, and the production of numerous publications, including the *Journal of Country Music*. It was the Country Music Foundation that gathered together this galaxy of country music chefs and asked them to tell a little about themselves and their culinary experiences.

Of course, a book like this could not have been produced without the cooperation of a lot of other good people, too. Our sincere thanks go out to the managers and publicists of all the stars who contributed to this book.

And thanks to you, the readers, for supporting country music. Bon appetit!

Bill Ivey
Director, Country Music Foundation

Introduction

By Anne Byrn
Food Editor of the Atlanta Journal/Constitution and Native of Nashville

Just as the lyrics of country music describe courtship, worship and hard work — all aspects of life in rural and urban America — the recipes loved by singers of these groups, too, are honest American fare.

After all, what really better soothes an aching soul than the rhythm of a country tune, a slice of hot cornbread and a bowl of homemade vegetable soup?

Country music singers are no different than you and me in that they need the comforts of home cooking on and off the road. Most of them were raised on it, and when they were asked to submit their favorite recipes, most stars sent recipes prepared by their loved ones. Charlie Daniels adores his wife's chocolate layer cake; Conway Twitty submitted his wife Mickey's baked ham with peach glaze.

The recipes aren't fancy. Outside of a pot of stew simmering for hours on the back burner, they don't take a lot of time to prepare. And, they don't use ingredients you wouldn't normally find in the average kitchen.

But not all country music is simple. It has twangs of honky tonk and Western swing. The stars' recipes, too, aren't all simple and homey. Tanya Tucker and Michael Martin Murphey, for example, prefer the hot spiciness of Mexican cooking.

Nashville grew as a major business and recording center for country music in the 1950s — about the time I was born. Growing up in Nashville, we always felt the presence of country music even if we lived miles away from the studios and didn't meet the stars face to face. It filled our air waves and changed our skyline. In the last 20 years the industry has really grown. The music still has the emotion and simplicity, but the sounds are more modern.

I still like country music, and a Saturday afternoon working around the house in Atlanta just wouldn't be the same without the radio spilling forth songs from Hank Williams, Jr., Dolly Parton and Kenny Rogers.

Likewise, pleasant family meals in Atlanta or Nashville aren't the same without the comforting foods that these stars hold special.

Anne Byrn

Mark Herndon, drummer for Alabama, likes to cook "when there is somebody to cook for." He remembers that, as a child, he was always told to "take all you want, but eat all you take" from the dinner table — so he eagerly complied and ate everything to show his appreciation.

Mark's father, a Marine pilot, kept the family traveling all over the country, so Mark got to sample many kinds of food. He claims to love Japanese food and seafood most, but jokes that his favorite meal is any meal that's free!

Mark plays a steady, up-tempo beat on the drums. Before joining Alabama in 1979, he played in circuit bands around his home in Myrtle Beach, South Carolina. He is happiest "playing the same arenas in South Carolina where I attended concerts a few years earlier," and has fond memories of a flight he once took with the Blue Angels. Hard to imagine that concert touring wouldn't provide enough excitement for Mark, but, yes, he expands his activities with flying and motorcycling, too!

The recipes Mark submitted for the cookbook are quick to fix, which we'd expect, given the fast pace Alabama follows. But once he settled down to a filling breakfast with Lionel Richie. As Mark describes it, Lionel prepared "eggs, sausages, biscuits and gravy — fixed the right way — heaped with the warmest hospitality west of the continental divide."

Considering the immense popularity of Alabama, Mark shouldn't be surprised to find warm hospitality wherever he goes.

Alabama's Mark Herndon

Deborah Allen likes to cook "occasionally," she says. But she'd much rather eat the home cooking of her mother, Rosetta Thurmond. She remembers that the meals her mother fixed back home in Memphis were "filled with love." To this day, Deborah says that Christmas dinner is always a very special mealtime, "because Mother fixes it, and it's always great. It's a very joyous occasion."

Good cooking is something of a tradition among the women in Deborah's family. One of her earliest memories of that tradition, Deborah recalls, was formed when she was a mischievous four-year-old: "I was visiting my Grandmother Posey, another wonderful cook. When she wasn't looking, I crawled up to the table and ate a big bowl of pork and beans before she could get the table set. Needless to say, I had a tummy ache."

As Deborah grew up, she found that cooking could be just as much an adventure as eating. "The first time I fixed a garlic dish with my nephew Shane," she recalls, "we put in too much garlic. We smelled like garlic for two days!" Since then Deborah has learned from her mistakes in the kitchen and she's a little more confident now, as her recipes show. Still, her favorite meal of all is a simple breakfast of Wheat Chex!

Up until a couple of years ago, Deborah had had her greatest professional success singing two overdubbed duets with the late Jim Reeves in 1979, and writing hits for Janie Fricke, Tammy Wynette, Tanya Tucker, Diana Ross and Sheena Easton. Then in 1983, she recorded "Baby, I Lied." The song was a surprise smash that climbed to #4 on the country charts and crossed over to become a pop hit, as well. As a result, Deborah was nominated for two Grammys. In early 1985, she released *Let Me Be The First* – the first digitally recorded lp to come out of Nashville. Deborah shares her recent good fortune with Nashville songwriter Rafe VanHoy, whom she met in 1978 and married four years later. They co-wrote "Baby, I Lied" (with Rory Bourke) and most of *Let Me Be the First*. Rafe produced the album.

Collaboration seems to come easily to the couple. Take their two-story colonial house in Nashville as an example: Rafe did the carpentry, while Deborah handled the wallpaper and decorating. When it comes to meals, they have a comfortable give-and-take arrangement worked out there, too. "We usually have lots of Chicken-I-Don't-Know," Deborah kids. "We know we're going to have chicken, but we don't know how it's going to be cooked." One thing is certain: Deborah will do the cooking. She does it, she says, "to show Rafe I love him." What happens when she doesn't feel like cooking? Then Rafe takes her out to a favorite Nashville restaurant like Houston's or Miss Daisy's, Deborah says, "so he can show me he loves me, too."

Bill Anderson likes to cook when he gets the chance. "I'm basically a creative person, and I think cooking is part of the creative process," he says. "I just wish I had more time to devote to learning about cooking." He generally finds time to eat, though. Asked to name his favorite cook, he replies, "It's a tie between my wife and my mother (I'm also a part-time politician!)." And his favorite meal? "Martha White Corn Meal (I'm also a part-time comedian)." Becoming a little more serious for a moment, Bill explains, "I don't have a favorite food. I usually like whatever I'm eating at the time. I'm not a picky eater at all. Mama always said, 'Clean your plate,' and I always did. I think that's one reason I like so many varied foods today. I had to eat what was put in front of me."

Sometimes he may not be picky *enough* about the food he eats. "With the schedule I'm on when I'm touring," he explains, "I'm ashamed to say, but I usually eat whatever is available."

Born in Columbia, South Carolina, Bill grew up in Georgia with an early love of music. He likes to say that he learned how to tune in a radio station before he learned to tie his shoes; he formed his first country band while still in high school. At the University of Georgia he earned a degree in journalism, intending to be a sportswriter. He did work for a couple of newspapers for a little while, but he was also working on songwriting. In 1958, Ray Price recorded Bill's "City Lights." The song went to #1 on the country chart, and Bill Anderson soon had a new career.

Bill estimates that he has written over 500 songs. Some of his best remembered hits are "Still," "Po Folks," and "Mama Sang a Song." He joined the Grand Ole Opry in 1961. Not only is he a well-respected tunesmith and singer, but he is also a well-known TV personality, having hosted his own syndicated country show for many years. Today he is the host of The Nashville Network's country trivia show "Fandango" and has made appearances on the daytime soap opera "One Life to Live." He is also the co-producer of The Nashville Network's "You Can Be a Star" showcase.

In addition to all of his entertainment business, Bill is a shareholder and spokesman for the Po Folks national restaurant chain. The chain is named after Bill's hit song, but Bill didn't become involved with the company until six years after it was founded. "My most memorable meal was the first time I ever ate at a Po Folks restaurant – memorable because I liked it so much I went out and bought part of the company!" he recalls. Being a shareholder in a restaurant chain makes it difficult for Bill to name one favorite restaurant. "There are 175 Po Folks restaurants," he says. "I can't single out any particular one or I'd have 174 people standing in line to swat me." He can admit, though, what his favorite meal in a restaurant is: "Pages One through Four from the menu at Po Folks!"

When Bill isn't busy with one of his careers, he enjoys life with wife Becky and son Jamey on their 35-acre farm outside Nashville. (Bill also has two college-age daughters, Teri and Jenni.) He remembers that his meals growing up in Georgia were "a pleasant time mostly with lots of conversation and family visiting. I try to carry that over into my family today – a relaxed time, a happy time, and each meal preceded by a family blessing to thank the Lord for our food and His grace."

Bill says he chose the recipes that he included in this book, because "they were easy to type. And they also included some of my favorite things to eat."

Bill Anderson

Bobby Bare

Bobby Bare is comfortable enough in the kitchen to have recorded an album in 1974 with his family called *Singin' in the Kitchen*. He also cooks for himself from time to time. Why? "So I can eat the things I like," he replies. After all, he is his own favorite cook.

But Bobby is even more at home in the recording studio, where, since 1962, he has made such memorable hits as "Detroit City," "500 Miles," and "Pour Me Another Tequila, Sheila." In fact, a recording studio was the set for his acclaimed cable TV talk show "Bobby Bare and Friends," where the laid-back, humorous Bare talked and sang with country music's best singers and songwriters.

The chart-topping records and TV stardom Bobby has achieved in Nashville seem a long way from the dirt-poor boyhood he had in the mining country on the Ohio-Kentucky border. Young Bobby worked on farms, as a bundle boy in a clothing factory and as an ice cream peddler. He also worked at music, but that was a labor of love. He learned to play the guitar at 11 and took to singing all the time, with or without the guitar. At 16, he left home at his father's insistence and fronted his own honky tonk band in Ohio. Later, he hitchhiked to California, joined the Army for two years, and played a bit part in a movie before making it in Nashville on his own terms.

Holidays never were a time of plenty in the Bare household, when Bobby was a child. "He never had a Christmas tree until we were married," his wife Jeannie once told *People* magazine. Small wonder, then, that Bobby says he doesn't much care for holiday meals. "I don't like turkey," he says, adding wryly, "I like turkey sandwiches."

Of childhood meals in general, Bobby says, "All I remember is biscuits and gravy, beans and taters and cornbread, day in and day out, every year." You might expect that he would avoid that kind of food now, but he doesn't: "I eat anything I want," he says, "and I still eat biscuits and gravy, beans and taters and cornbread." He also eats "a good steak, loaded with garlic, oysters on the half shell, linguine with white clam sauce," when he dines out. His favorite restaurant for elegant dining is Mario's in Nashville.

Nevertheless, Bobby says he likes eating breakfast best of all. In fact, one of his most memorable meals was spent at the breakfast table at the Playboy Mansion with his good friend and frequent collaborator, cartoonist/songwriter Shel Silverstein. They had sausage and eggs, as Bobby recalls.

Bobby also likes cheeseburgers and pasta dishes, with cheeseburgers being the food he eats most often on the road. Asked why he chose the recipes included in this cookbook, he replies in typically straightforward, amusing, Bare fashion: "I didn't; my wife did."

In 1984, Earl Thomas Conley's third album, *Don't Make It Easy For Me*, produced four singles that went to #1 on the country charts. No other artist in any genre has duplicated that feat.

But success hasn't changed the smokey-voiced singer who's been called "the thinking man's country artist." He still lives in a modest home in Nashville with Sandra, his wife of more than 22 years, and their children. Sometimes Earl will cook for himself, though he prefers Sandra's cooking by far. She's his favorite cook.

Like his music, his taste in food is straightforward, yet sophisticated. He says his favorite meal of the day is lunch and his favorite dish is a hearty bowl of beef stew. But when he and Sandra eat out, Earl likes to order oysters on the half shell and baked flounder. He's also a big fan of Italian food; his favorite Nashville restaurant, in fact, is Ciraco's.

One of eight children of a railroad worker, young Earl grew up in Portsmouth, Ohio. He started out aspiring to be an actor, then to be a painter and a sculptor. Clearly, from an early age he wanted an audience, and deserved one. But he was headstrong, too. He received a scholarship to art school and turned it down to hitchhike to Colorado with a buddy. Afterwards, Earl joined the Army and spent two years stationed in West Germany. While in the service, he learned to play the guitar and began tinkering with songwriting.

It wasn't until 1968, though, that he took the craft seriously. By that time he had been married to Sandra, his high school sweetheart, for a few years and had two children. After an abortive attempt to break into the music business in Nashville, Earl and the family moved to Huntsville, Alabama. There, he worked in a steel mill and kept at the songs. In 1976, Conway Twitty, one of Earl's boyhood idols, took a song Earl co-wrote, "This Time I've Hurt Her More Than She Loves Me," to #1. Earl Thomas Conley was on his way.

Now he's a big enough star to say he's had dinner with Dolly Parton and play the matter down. "We had roast duck" is all he says about it. He credits his family for his stability. "It helps my music," he once told columnist Jack Hurst, "to still come from a family orientation. Otherwise, I think I would be too much of a performer, not serious enough to be a good writer or a good anything else." After a laugh, he added, "It keeps me out of trouble."

Earl would be the first to admit that these recipes, some of his favorites, help keep him out of trouble, too.

Earl Thomas Conley

Helen Cornelius

Helen Cornelius enjoys cooking almost as much as she does performing . . . except for the time "I ruined a six-pound eye of tenderloin roast! Cooking seems to release me from tension," says the petite (5′ ½″), energetic singer. She particularly likes to cook during the holidays. "Christmas and Thanksgiving are always memorable to me," she admits. "I love the food and the occasions they represent. My family and I are together then, and I cook all of their favorites."

During the rest of the year, Helen's own favorite from the kitchen is fried chicken, served with mashed potatoes and gravy, fresh snap beans, spinach salad, fresh fruit and iced tea. "I enjoy all types of Southern cooking," she says, "but I also like health food recipes. I make very few sweets, except at Christmas, because I'm interested in cooking dishes that are tasty, but also good for you."

Helen grew up in a family of eight on a 140-acre farm outside Hannibal, Missouri. She remembers their meals as "regular — a big breakfast, lunch and then a large supper. We had lots of fresh vegetables, home-canned fruits and jellies and home-made breads." Her favorite contribution to the table back then was cookies. "I always made sugar cookies — the kind where you chill the dough, roll it out real thin, sprinkle with sugar, and then bake. I always took them to our youth meetings at church, and I really took pride in making them."

Now Helen can take pride in her singing career. For four and a half years, she teamed up with Jim Ed Brown to record such memorable duets as "I Don't Want to Have to Marry You" and "Don't Bother to Knock." In 1977, Helen and Jim Ed won the CMA's Vocal Duo of the Year award. But that was only the beginning for Helen. Since 1981, she has gone solo and in 1984, she earned glowing reviews for her role as Annie Oakley in a road-show revival of Irving Berlin's *Annie Get Your Gun.*

Helen has come a long way from singing on the front porch with her family, but not so far that she doesn't still appreciate the down home fare of her favorite Nashville restaurant, Dotson's. Helen says they serve "fried chicken, all kinds of vegetables, corn bread and the *best ever* home-made pies." . . . To one of the best country talents!

Charlie Daniels has an unusual definition of a bad meal: he says it's "any meal when I'm on a diet." Since he began fighting the battle of the bulge a couple of years ago, the 6'4", 240-pound singer has had a lot more "bad" meals than he used to. Still, he thinks it's worth the trouble. "It's not an image change," he says. "It's for my health. I try to watch what I eat because I feel better when I'm a little lighter. The doctor likes it a whole lot better, too."

It's no wonder, though, that Charlie looks forward to traditional meals like Thanksgiving and Christmas every year. At Christmas dinner especially, he jokes, "I can eat too much and not feel guilty."

Charlie, who doesn't cook for himself, says his favorite cook is his wife, Hazel. He's been savoring her home-cooked meals for over 20 years now. His favorite food, he says, is her "soul food," and his favorite meal is her country-style steak and rice. On the road, where he's at the mercy of truckstops and fast food franchises, Charlie says, "I often eat things I shouldn't be eating."

Charlie grew up in Wilmington, North Carolina, the only child of a timberman and his wife. He remembers that meals back then were "basic," and he has fond memories of the breakfasts of grits and eggs that his mother used to fix.

Charlie started playing music when he was 15. His first love was bluegrass, but in his late teens he heard Elvis Presley's first records and they made a big impression on him. For the next several years, he toured the country in journeyman bands until the late '60s, when he was offered session work in Nashville. He soon made a name for himself backing Bob Dylan, Flatt and Scruggs, and Ringo Starr in Nashville recording sessions.

When he set out on the road again in the early '70s, he had a new band and a renewed confidence in his own brand of rocking country music. Since then, he's had big hits with "The South's Gonna Do It Again," "In America" and "The Devil Went Down to Georgia," as well as many others.

Charlie loves touring and playing onstage with his buddies in the band. But he also enjoys time off at home with his wife and son, Charlie, on their 350-acre farm in Mt. Juliet, Tennessee, where they raise quarterhorses and cattle. "I guess if I've got any kind of hobby," he once told *People* magazine, "it's horses. Country boys just like to ride. I started doing it for pleasure a few years ago, but now I've found it's a real need. It's a way for me to get completely away from things for a while."

Of course, good food is a preoccupation of his, too. A meal for him, Charlie says, "varies from very simple when I'm on a diet to very fancy." A fancy meal for him is lobster, which he likes to eat when he dines out. Asked to name his most memorable meal, Charlie says it has to be the time he had quesadillas with western novelist Louis L' Amour.

With all the varieties of food that Charlie likes, why did he include chocolate cake as his recipe? "Because," he says, "I love chocolate cake!"

Soups and Salads

TANYA TUCKER'S
CHEESE AND POTATO SOUP

"I like to spice my bowl of Cheese-potato soup with a dash of Crystal Louisiana Red Sauce," Tanya tells us.

4	cups water
3	cups potatoes, peeled and diced
1	carrot, grated
1	onion, finely chopped
1	head fresh broccoli (optional), chopped into bite-size pieces
¼	cup butter
¼	cup flour
2	cups milk
¾	16-ounce block Velveeta cheese, cut into chunks
	Salt and pepper
1	clove garlic, mashed

In large saucepan, combine water, potatoes, carrot, onion and broccoli (if desired). Boil until just tender. Drain.

In bottom of double boiler, boil water. In top of double boiler, combine butter and flour and stir to make a paste. Add milk and cook, stirring constantly, until thickened and smooth. Add cheese, a few chunks at a time, to milk mixture. When thickened and all cheese is melted, add to potato mixture and blend well. Add salt, pepper and garlic to taste.

Makes 6 to 8 servings.

Editors Note: You may wish to use fewer potatoes when including broccoli.

BOBBY BARE'S POTATO AND CHEESE SOUP

A soup that is particularly good on a cold winter's day.

1	10¾ can cream of potato soup
2	¼ inch- thick slices Velveeta cheese
2	strips crisply-cooked bacon
	Bacon drippings (optional)

Place undiluted cream of potato soup in saucepan. Add Velveeta cheese. Crumble bacon on top of soup and heat all together until cheese is melted and soup is hot. Stir well. Add bacon drippings for flavor if desired.

Makes 2 servings.

THE STATLER BROTHERS' DIET VEGETABLE SOUP

This soup is an excellent diet food. The vegetables are low in calories and the broth fills you up.

2 cups tomato juice
1 cup chopped cabbage
½ cup green beans, cut in 1" pieces
½ cup diced celery
1 medium tomato, peeled and coarsely diced
½ cup sliced carrots
2 parsnips, pared and diced
1 small onion, chopped
1 ½-ounce packet instant vegetable broth and seasoning mix
1 chicken or beef bouillion cube

Combine all ingredients in a large saucepan and simmer uncovered for 1 to 2 hours or until tender. Add water if broth becomes too thick.

Makes 4 to 6 servings.

HANK WILLIAMS, JR.'S COUNTRY-STYLE VEGETABLE AND BEEF SOUP

When Hank is spending time at his Alabama home, he enjoys this for lunch or dinner.

1½ pounds ground or chopped beef or stew meat
12 black peppercorns (optional)
4 quarts water
2 onions, chopped
1 16-ounce can tomatoes, cut up
1 15-ounce can tomato sauce
2 cups diced potatoes
2 carrots, sliced
2 ribs celery, sliced
1 10-ounce package frozen green beans
1 10-ounce package frozen baby lima beans
1 10-ounce package frozen corn
  Salt and pepper to taste
1 cup egg noodles
1 cup elbow or shell macaroni

Simmer meat with peppercorns, if desired, in water in large covered pot for 1½ hours. Remove from heat. Skim. Remove peppercorns.

Add onions, tomatoes, tomato sauce and bring to boil. Reduce heat and cook 1 hour more. Add potatoes and all vegtables and cook 45 minutes more. Add salt and pepper to taste. Add noodles and macaroni and cook until the noodles are done. If desired, thin with V-8 juice, water, broth or tomato juice.

Makes 8 to 12 servings.

Editors Note: Fresh vegetables may be used in place of frozen. Use 1 pound of green beans cut into 1-inch pieces, 1 pound lima beans, shelled, and corn from 3 to 4 ears.

HELEN CORNELIUS' HOMEMADE CHICKEN SOUP

The old-fashioned recipe your grandmother recommended as the perfect remedy for all ills.

1	5- to 6-pound hen
5	quarts water
1	bay leaf
1	large onion, chopped
2	tablespoons salt
½	cup finely diced carrots
½	cup finely diced celery
	Sprinkle of diced parsley
2	cups egg noodles or ¾ cup rice, uncooked

Stew hen in 6-quart pot with water, bay leaf, onion and salt. Cover, bring to boil; turn heat to low and simmer until tender, about 2 hours. Remove lid from pot and let hen cool in cooking liquid. Pick good meat off bones and cut into small pieces. Discard skin and bones.

Strain broth and add chicken pieces, carrots, celery and parsley. "Depending on what I have on hand, I either add egg noodles or rice — more or less of either, depending on whether you like mostly broth or not."

Bring to a boil. Turn heat to medium and cook until rice or noodles are tender.

Makes approximately 5 quarts.

TOM T. HALL'S WILTED LETTUCE SALAD

Tom T. says that this unusual salad is "best when served with mashed potatoes on top of it . . . but it may be served any way you choose!"

1	bunch leaf lettuce, shredded
1	bunch radishes, tops removed and sliced
1	bunch green onions, chopped
3	strips bacon
	Bacon drippings

In mixing bowl, toss lettuce, radishes and onions.

Fry bacon until crisp. Drain bacon; reserve drippings. Crumble bacon into salad and toss. Immediately prior to serving, heat bacon drippings and pour over salad to wilt lettuce.

Makes 4 to 6 servings.

T. G. SHEPPARD'S SIX LAYER GREEN SALAD

Layered salads are very attractive and a different twist on tossed salads.

1   small head lettuce, chopped
1   16-ounce can green peas, drained
1   medium onion, chopped
1   cup Miracle Whip salad dressing
1   cup shredded Swiss cheese
½   cup bacon bits

Layer all ingredients in a large bowl in the order given above. Do not toss. Marinate covered in the refrigerator for at least five hours.

Makes 10 servings.

Editors Note: Approximately 2 cups of shelled fresh English peas, cooked, may replace canned peas.

HELEN CORNELIUS' GREEN SALAD
WITH CLASSIC DRESSING

Helen is especially interested in healthy recipes and this salad fills the bill.

1   head lettuce
1   medium cucumber, thinly sliced
1   small purple onion, thinly sliced
8   cherry tomatoes, halved
1   green pepper
1   tablespoon plus 1 teaspoon vegetable oil
½   teaspoon salt
    Dash garlic powder
    Dash pepper
2   teaspoons wine vinegar
3   hard-boiled eggs, crumbled

Tear lettuce into bite-size pieces and place in a salad bowl. Add cucumber, onion, tomatoes and green pepper. When ready to serve, sprinkle with oil; toss until lettuce glistens. Season with salt, garlic powder and pepper. Sprinkle with vinegar. Toss until lettuce is well-coated.

Divide into 4 serving bowls. Sprinkle each with eggs.

Makes 4 servings.

THE OAK RIDGE BOYS' HEARTS OF MINE SALAD

Serve this elegant salad as an appetizer or salad course for a special meal. This recipe comes from a fan of the Oak Ridge Boys, Mrs. Ruby Sellars.

2   14-ounce cans artichoke hearts, drained
1   14-ounce can hearts of palm, drained and cut in half
2   cups small fresh brussel sprouts, cooked
¼   cup vinegar
½   cup vegetable oil
1   small clove garlic, minced
1   tablespoon sugar
1   teaspoon salt
    Dash hot pepper sauce
1   tablespoon minced onion

Place artichoke hearts, hearts of palm and brussel sprouts in a bowl.

In separate bowl, combine remaining ingredients for the marinade and pour over the vegetables. Toss lightly.

Cover and place in refrigerator overnight. Serve cold.

Makes 6 servings.

RAYMONE'S SALAD

Try this full-of-vegetables salad by Ray Stevens with the Statler Brothers' recipe for Easy French Bread, page 71, for lunch or a light dinner.

Salad
½   head romaine lettuce, torn into bite-size pieces
½   head Iceberg lettuce, torn into bite-size pieces
3   small onions, chopped
1   bell pepper, chopped
1   14-ounce can artichoke hearts, drained
1   14-ounce can asparagus tips. drained
4   radishes, sliced
1   large tomato, chopped
1   carrot, sliced
2   ribs celery, chopped
2   hard cooked eggs, sliced
1   cup Flav-O-Rich cottage cheese
½   cup sliced sweet pickles
¼   cup India relish
⅛   cup bacon bits

Dressing
2   tablespoons bottled avocado dressing
2   tablespoons bottled blue cheese dressing
2   tablespoons bottled thousand island dressing

Gently toss all salad ingredients together in large bowl. Mix bottled dressings and add to salad. Toss well and serve immediately.

Makes 6 to 8 servings.

THE OAK RIDGE BOYS' BROCCOLI SALAD

Submitted for your culinary pleasure by Susan Golden, William Lee's daughter-in-law.

2	heads fresh broccoli
4	hard-cooked eggs, chopped
½	cup chopped green olives
½	onion, grated
1	cup sliced fresh mushrooms
1	cup mayonnaise
1	tablespoon lemon juice
½	teaspoon sugar
	Lettuce leaves (optional)

Wash broccoli and remove tough stems. Chop flowerets and remaining stems into 1-inch pieces.

Mix all ingredients together and chill.

Serve on lettuce leaves, if desired.

Makes 8 servings.

THE JUDDS' KRAUT SALAD

Try this with pork or ham. It is simply delicious.

1	quart sauerkraut
1	onion, minced
1	green pepper, minced
3	ribs celery, minced
2	cups sugar
1	2-ounce jar chopped pimentos, drained

Mix all ingredients together and store in a glass jar at least 1 day before serving. Stores up to 3 weeks in the refrigerator.

Makes 4 servings.

THE WHITES' SAUERKRAUT SALAD

A wonderfully spicy favorite of Sharon White; when you try it, it will be a favorite of yours, too.

1	16-ounce can kraut
1	cup sugar
½	cup vinegar
1	2-ounce jar diced pimentos, drained
½	cup chopped onion
1	cup finely chopped green pepper
1	cup finely chopped celery
1	8-ounce can diced carrots, drained

Drain sauerkraut, reserving liquid. Combine liquid from sauerkraut with sugar and vinegar in a saucepan. Boil 2 minutes. Place all vegetables in a bowl. Pour liquid over vegetables. Mix well. Cover and store overnight in fridge. When ready to serve, stir well.

Makes 6 to 8 servings.

BARBARA MANDRELL'S MARINATED BEAN SALAD

A nice thing about Barbara's recipe — it is made the day before serving . . . a big help for a busy person.

1   8-ounce can small English peas, drained
1   16-ounce can French-cut green beans, drained
1   8-ounce can water chestnuts, drained
1   cup chopped celery
1   cup chopped bell pepper
1   large onion, chopped
8   cherry tomatoes

Marinade
1   cup water
1   cup vegetable oil
1   cup vinegar
½   cup sugar

Place all vegetables in a large bowl. Toss.

Mix marinade ingredients and pour over vegetables. Cover tightly. Marinate overnight in refrigerator. Toss well; drain off the liquid when ready to serve.

Makes 8 to 10 servings.

Editors Note: Fresh peas and green beans may be used for this recipe in place of canned. Shell enough peas to make 1 cup and cook until tender. Remove tips from 1 pound of green beans, cut and blanch 4 to 5 minutes.

CONWAY TWITTY'S THREE-BEAN SALAD

Conway says that "everybody seems to have a favorite three-bean salad recipe, but this one is different. The secret is Dr. Pepper."

1   16-ounce can each French-cut green beans, yellow wax beans and kidney beans
½   cup vinegar
1   tablespoon sugar
¼   cup vegetable oil
¼   cup Dr. Pepper
    Salt and pepper to taste
1   red onion, thinly sliced and separated into rings

Drain all the beans well. Combine vinegar, sugar, oil, Dr. Pepper, salt and pepper in a jar. Shake vigorously.

Place the drained vegetables and onion rings in a bowl. Pour the dressing over them and toss lightly. Cover tightly and refrigerate for a few hours or overnight. Toss occasionally during standing time and just before serving.

"Makes a big bowl!" (12 or more servings).

Editors Note: Fresh green and yellow wax beans are very good in this recipe. You may substitute one pound of each, cooked, drained and cut in 1" pieces.

TOM T. HALL'S GUACAMOLE SALAD

Tom serves this two ways . . . on a bed of lettuce as a salad or in a bowl with tortilla chips as a dip.

2   *ripe avocados, peeled and quartered*
½   *fresh lemon*
1   *large white onion, finely chopped*
1   *large ripe tomato, finely chopped*
     Salt and pepper

Place avocados in blender container. Squeeze juice from lemon over avocados. Blend with onion until creamy smooth. Add tomato and salt and pepper to taste. Blend thoroughly. Chill until ready to serve.

Makes 4 servings.

TANYA TUCKER'S GUACAMOLE SALAD

"I like to cook fresh corn tortillas in ¼ cup of oil in a skillet until crisp," Tanya tells us. "Drain on paper towels and sprinkle with salt, pepper and garlic salt."

3   *ripe avocados, peeled, mashed*
1   *ripe tomato, diced*
3   *green onions, white part only, finely diced*
2   *fresh cloves garlic, finely diced or pressed*
     Hot sauce or salsa to taste
     Salt and pepper to taste
     Corn tortillas

In a bowl, mash avocados; add tomatoes, green onions and garlic. Mix thoroughly. Add hot sauce or salsa, salt and pepper to taste. Mix well. Serve with corn tortillas.

Makes 2 to 4 servings.

THE WHITES' SLAW

"A slaw freezes well," says Sharon White. Before you freeze it, let the slaw set for 24 hours in the refrigerator. Be sure to thaw before serving."

2   *cups sugar*
½-⅔ *cup vinegar*
2   *teaspoons salt*
½   *tablespoon mustard seed*
½   *tablespoon celery seed*
1   *large head cabbage, shredded*
1   *large green pepper, finely chopped*
1   *small onion, finely chopped*

In saucepan, combine sugar, vinegar, salt and mustard and celery seeds. Place over low heat, stirring occasionally, until sugar melts. Cool.

Toss cabbage, green pepper and onion in large bowl. Pour cooled sauce over slaw. Toss well. Let slaw stand 24 hours in refrigerator before serving.

Makes 6 to 8 servings.

DOLLY PARTON'S COLE SLAW

The pickle juice adds a special tang to Dolly's slaw.

1	medium head cabbage, chopped
1	medium onion, finely chopped
1	carrot, chopped or grated
½	bell pepper, finely chopped
2	teaspoons sugar
¼	teaspoon black pepper
1	teaspoon salt
¼	cup sweet pickle juice
¼	cup white vinegar
1	dill pickle, chopped, or 1 tablespoon pickle relish
1	cup mayonnaise

Mix all ingredients in large bowl.

Refrigerate until ready to serve.

Makes 10 to 12 servings.

REBA McENTIRE'S POKE SALAD DELIGHT

Reba recommends you know the source of the poke greens, being "sure to pick greens that have not been sprayed with insecticides or any other chemicals." Poke is sold mostly in the South and in Pennsylvania Dutch country and is a native American green.

1	grocery sack poke greens, approximately 3 pounds
1	medium onion, diced
4	tablespoons butter or margarine
1	pound ground beef
	Salt and pepper to taste
6	eggs, beaten

Pick a grocery sack full of poke greens. "Pick mainly the leaves — a few stalks are okay. Do not pick plants more than 2 feet high or with thin stalks." Wash thoroughly and drain.

In large kettle, parboil poke greens in water to cover, about 10 minutes. Drain and parboil a second time. Drain.

Brown onion in skillet with 2 tablespoons butter or margarine. Add ground beef, seasoned to taste, and brown over medium heat. Drain off fat.

In separate skillet, melt remaining 2 tablespoons butter and scramble eggs. Mix greens, beef mixture and eggs in serving dish "and eat."

Makes 6 to 8 servings.

Editors Note: Parboiling is partially cooking food in water before completing cooking in another way such as frying.

KENNY ROGERS' COUNTRY CHICKEN SALAD

As Kenny will tell you, he doesn't consider himself a gourmet cook, but he makes a great chicken salad — and this is it!

2   cups chopped cooked chicken
1   cup chopped apple
4   hard-cooked eggs, chopped
½   cup Kraft mayonnaise
¼   cup sweet pickle relish, drained
     Slivered toasted almonds (optional)

Combine all ingredients except almonds; mix lightly. Chill. When serving, garnish with almonds, if desired.

Makes 4 servings.

HELEN CORNELIUS' CURRIED CHICKEN SALAD

If you love curry, you may never go back to plain chicken salad after trying this one.

1   cup plain yogurt
1   cup mayonnaise
1   teaspoon curry powder
1   large onion, chopped
2   pounds cooked chicken, skinned, boned and diced
1   cup chopped walnuts
1   cup raisins
     Romaine lettuce leaves
     Chopped parsley

Combine yogurt, mayonnaise and curry powder in a large bowl. Add onion, chicken, walnuts and raisins; toss. Refrigerate for two hours or longer. Serve on lettuce leaves and sprinkle with parsley.

Makes 4 to 6 servings.

MICHAEL MARTIN MURPHEY'S POTATO SALAD

This potato salad recipe comes compliments of "Mama Murphey," Michael's mother.

8-10 medium potatoes, peeled
1   cup chopped celery
1   cup finely chopped sweet pickles (or use sweet relish)
6   hard-boiled eggs, chopped
1   cup chopped apples (optional)
½   cup chopped pecans
1   cup sour cream
1   cup mayonnaise
2   tablespoons prepared mustard
      Salt and pepper to taste

Boil potatoes until just done. Let cool and cut into cubes. Add celery, relish, eggs, apples if desired, and pecans. Mix sour cream, mayonnaise and mustard until blended and add to potato mixture. Add salt and pepper to taste.

Makes 8 servings.

THE OAK RIDGE BOYS' LAYERED POTATO SALAD

This salad is prettiest served in a large glass bowl but tasty no matter what type of bowl you use.

½   head green cabbage, shredded
½   head red cabbage, shredded
10   medium cooked potatoes, peeled and sliced
    Salt, pepper, celery seed
3 or 4 medium onions, sliced
3   bell peppers, sliced
5   hard-boiled eggs, chopped
1   quart mayonnaise
    Paprika

Place a layer of each cabbage in bottom of deep bowl. Place a layer of potatoes on top of the cabbage. Sprinkle with salt, pepper, and celery seed to taste. Add a layer of onions, peppers and eggs. Spread layer of mayonnaise over these ingredients. Repeat layers. Sprinkle paprika over top.

Makes 12 servings.

PEE WEE KING'S BAKED GERMAN POTATO SALAD

German potato salad is usually served warm but is very good cold, too.

1   cup diced bacon
1   cup diced celery
1   cup chopped onion
3   tablespoons salt (or less to taste)
3   tablespoons flour
⅔   cup sugar
⅔   cup vinegar
½   teaspoon pepper
1⅓ cup water
8   cups cooked and peeled potatoes, sliced

Fry bacon and drain, reserving drippings.

Preheat oven to 350 degrees.

Return 4 tablespoons drippings to skillet. Add celery, onion salt and flour. Cook over medium heat, stirring gently until golden. Add sugar, vinegar, pepper and water. Bring to boil. Place sliced potatoes and bacon pieces in a 3-quart baking dish. Pour mixture over potatoes.

Cover and bake for 30 minutes.

Makes 12 servings.

THE OAK RIDGE BOYS' PRETZEL SALAD

This unusual salad is at its best when allowed to set for 24 hours before serving. It also would make an interesting dessert.

2	cups crushed pretzels
¾	cup butter, melted
1	tablespoon sugar
1	8-ounce package cream cheese
1	cup sugar
1	8-ounce carton Cool Whip
2	cups pineapple juice
2	3-ounce packages strawberry Jell-O
2	10-ounce packages frozen strawberries
	lettuce leaves (optional)

Preheat oven to 350 degrees.

Mix pretzels, melted butter and sugar and press into 9 by 13-inch baking pan. Bake 6 to 10 minutes. Let cool completely.

Blend cream cheese and sugar in bowl. Add Cool Whip. Spread mixture over cooled pretzel crust.

In saucepan, heat pineapple juice to boiling. Add Jell-O. Stir until dissolved. Add frozen berries. Stir. Pour over cheese mixture and let set in refrigerator. Cut into squares. Serve on bed of lettuce if desired.

Makes 12 servings.

BOBBY BARE'S FRUIT SALAD

If colored miniature marshmallows are not available, substitute small white ones.

4	medium Red Delicious apples
3	medium bananas
½	6-ounce bottle maraschino cherries, drained and chopped
½	cup chopped walnuts
1	cup Tokay (red seedless) grapes, halved
8	ounces colored miniature marshmallows
1	8-ounce container whipped topping
1	teaspoon mayonnaise
	Dash sugar (to suit own taste)
1	small head Iceberg lettuce (optional)

Peel and core apples, chop into bite-size pieces and place in mixing bowl. Peel bananas, slice and add to apples. Add cherries, walnuts, grapes and marshmallows. Mix.

Add whipped topping, mayonnaise and sugar to taste. Mix gently. Serve over lettuce, if desired.

Makes 6 servings.

Editors Note: If you prefer to use fresh whipped cream, whip until stiff ½ pint heavy cream and substitute for whipped topping.

Little Jimmy Dickens may be small (4' 11"), but it's not for lack of interest in food. He enjoys a good meal and he cooks for himself when he has the chance. "Yes, I do enjoy cooking," he says. "I find that being creative in the kitchen is not unlike creating music. In each case, I start with raw material and attempt to create something meaningful."

When he wants to eat something really meaningful, though, he turns to his favorite cook — his wife, Miss Mona — to fix it. "My favorite food is a dish of Southern pot roast," he says. When he goes out to eat, he likes to order prime ribs of beef well done. But even now, after nearly 40 years of stardom, he still finds that he doesn't often have time to linger over his meals. "Unfortunately," he says, "we often eat at fast food restaurants to save time in meeting hectic schedules."

Jimmy's schedule has been hectic for a long time. The oldest in a family of 13 children in Bolt, West Virginia, Little Jimmy started performing on local radio at age 15. He soon made a name for himself as the little fellow with the big voice. He joined the Grand Ole Opry in 1948 and, shortly afterward, began recording a string of hits including "Take an Old Cold Tater (and Wait)," "A-Sleepin' at the Foot of the Bed" and "I'm Little, But I'm Loud." His biggest hit came in 1965 when he recorded "May the Bird of Paradise Fly Up Your Nose," which went to #1. In 1964, Jimmy became the first country performer to make a complete circuit of the globe while on tour.

Being a star performer for nearly four decades has meant that Jimmy has been wined and dined by the biggest names in country music. "I have eaten with many famous people," he says, "such as Hank Williams, Roy Acuff, Ernest Tubb, Tennessee Governor Frank Clement and many, many others. I have had so many memorable meals with fine folks around the world that I cannot recall any one meal that ranks above all the others."

He still has fond memories, too, of mealtimes when he was growing up in a crowded household in Depression-era West Virginia. As he recalls, the meals "were very simple, but always enough. Today, the economy allows my family to eat a greater variety; however, we still stick to rather simple Southern food." He claims that one reason he enjoys the turkey during holiday meals so much is that "it brings back childhood memories."

Jimmy says he chose the three recipes included because they've been the most requested from his kitchen for many years.

Little Jimmy Dickens

Lee Greenwood

In 1975, if you'd shown up at the right fast food restaurant in California, Lee Greenwood would have been frying your chicken. Today, you'll have to content yourself with just his recipes. The CMA Male Vocalist of the Year for 1983 and 1984 has enough trouble finding time to cook for himself. And no wonder: his rough-around-the-edges tenor and his good looks have been turning womens' heads ever since he broke into the country charts and stayed for 22 weeks in 1981 with the single, "It Turns Me Inside Out."

Actually, Lee worked only briefly in fast food. For most of the last 20 years, he's been a professional musician, working the Nevada club circuit as a jack-of-all-trades: arranger, band leader, show tune writer, bass player and piano bar singer. It was in Las Vegas that Larry McFaden, Mel Tillis' longtime bass player and band leader, spotted Lee and persuaded him to come to Nashville to record some demos with Mel's band. The result was that Lee, who was already getting some attention as a songwriter, became a recording star.

Raised on his grandparents' small farm in Sacramento, California, Lee still has an appetite for down home fare, like pumpkin pie (his favorite dish), and fried chicken, sweet potatoes and cranberry sauce for the holidays. And as long as it's not fried chicken, he enjoys doing the cooking himself. "I like to keep the creative juices flowing, even when I'm at home," Lee says. "Usually I write songs, but to really relax, I take out my recipe file and cook something delicious."

Not that Lee's averse to a good restaurant meal. When he can, Lee likes to have dinner at The Summit on Lake Tahoe. A meal of escargot, Caesar salad, filet mignon or veal Oscar, broccoli or spinach and bananas flambé suits him just fine. Always the ladies' man, Lee is quick to point out that his favorite cook is still his wife, Melanie.

With songs like "The Ballad of Forty Dollars," "I Love" and "Old Dogs, Children, and Watermelon Wine," it's clear that Tom T. Hall has a keen, cock-eyed appreciation for the little things that most of us take for granted. Like his songs, his tales about mealtimes are also a little strange and funny.

He recalls, for example, the time his wife was invited to have lunch with First Lady Rosalyn Carter. "I tagged along," says Tom T. "Mrs. Carter had had the cooks prepare a quiche for the occasion. When I showed up, Mrs. Carter apologized for serving quiche to a man. I apologized for showing up at all — and enjoyed my quiche." Then there was the unforgettable meal at the truckstop. It was, he says, "the worst meal I ever had." What happened? "The cook ran out of cooking oil and turned to diesel fuel as a substitute."

Part of what makes Tom T. Hall an engaging storyteller and songwriter is a life that's rich in experiences. The son of a Kentucky preacher, young Tom dropped out of high school at 15 to work in a garment factory by day and perform bluegrass by night. Later, he joined the Army, served in Germany, and earned his high school diploma. In 1964, he moved to Nashville and soon proved to be such a prolific songwriter that he couldn't get all his songs recorded by other singers. So he began to record a few himself. "A Week in a Country Jail" went to #1 in 1968; "Harper Valley PTA" became a smash hit for Jeannie C. Riley.

Today, many hits and three books later, Tom T. lives on a 60-acre farm in Franklin, Tennessee. There, he says he likes to do a little woodworking and a little cooking, too. "I enjoy cooking in the wintertime, particularly," he says. "Then the office is closed, the phone is off the hook and there's plenty of time to make everything from scratch. Although I have no natural ability as a cook, I like to throw everything together the way the book says and see what comes out."

While Tom eats a lot of fish and chicken filets on the road ("They are plentiful and very little can be done to render such food completely inedible"), his favorite food is an unusual one: fresh lettuce. "I have a vegetable garden that I tend myself," Tom says. "The first thing ready to eat in the early spring is the lettuce and spring onions. I make these into a salad. That's my all-time favorite food." Naturally, the Storyteller also has an interesting comment on his favorite meal: frog legs, French style. "The big frog legs that are sold in stores and served at roadside seafood shops are not very good," he says. "But the smaller, more delicate, freshwater frogs are delicious in garlic butter sauce. While this food is difficult to find in the U.S.A., it is not a rarity in France." Maybe not, but characters (and cooks) like Tom T. Hall probably are!

Tom T. Hall

Emmylou Harris

When it comes to working in the kitchen, Emmylou Harris likes simplicity. In fact, she claims that she's "more at home in the woods with cornmeal, a campfire and an iron skillet. With all the modern conveniences, I just get by."

She believes in eating healthful food, but she's by no means a fanatic about it. During her pregnancy with her second child, Meghann, she says she began "sort of flirting with being a health food person, though I'm not dedicated enough." When Emmylou came down with prenatal indigestion, a nutritionist prescribed a grain and vegetable diet to ease her discomfort. "It worked," says Emmylou. "But I didn't expect the rest of the family to go along with my eating." About nutrition and diet in general she observes: "I think there's a certain point in your life where you have to start taking better care of yourself, or every aspect of your life is going to suffer because of it."

For Emmylou, taking care of herself and her daughters, Hallie and Meghann, included a move in 1983 from Los Angeles to Nashville. "There's a different feel to Nashville from Los Angeles," she explains. "This is a real family-oriented town. It's all right to be a mother here; you're not in the minority. A lot of my friends here are like me — with children — and the slower pace suits us."

The slower pace gives Emmylou a well-deserved respite from the rigors of traveling and recording, a rest she needs now that she is a bonafide, headlining country star. She first came to the attention of music fans in the early 70s through her duets with the late Gram Parsons, a pioneer of country rock. Up until that point, Emmylou had mainly been a folk music fan. But inspired by Parsons, she turned more and more to country music. In the 70s, she recruited Rodney Crowell and Ricky Skaggs for her Hot Band. Both men have since gone on to solo fame and fortune, but not before helping Emmylou to make music that has brought her Grammy awards for her *Blue Kentucky Girl* album and for her single "In My Dreams," and such hits as "Save the Last Dance for Me" and "Beneath Still Waters."

Another fruitful collaboration, with English songwriter Paul Kennerly, produced her 1985 critically-acclaimed country concept album, *The Ballad of Sally Rose*. Emmylou wrote or co-wrote all of the album's 13 tracks — the most songs she's ever contributed to one of her albums. In the course of that project, she came to realize that writing songs and being a mother is hard work. "I used to be able to hang out with the boys as good as anybody," she recently told *Country Music* magazine. "But now I have a hard time staying up to watch the reruns of 'Barney Miller.' When you get up at seven in morning to cook your kid's breakfast, and then spend the whole day in the studio, or writing, and then pick her up at school in the afternoon, fix supper, give her a bath and put her to bed, I'll tell ya somethin': when ten or eleven o'clock rolls around, you're ready for the sack!"

Christmas is a good time for Emmylou to whip up her mother's Broccoli-Nut Casserole. Emmylou admits that Eugenia Harris' dish "looks weird," but it's always a big hit. In fact, she says it's a treat for just about any holiday occasion. She remembers that it was a big favorite at a Fourth of July potluck party at Malibu held by her buddy, Linda Ronstadt. "They must have liked it," Emmylou says. "They ate it all up." Try it and see if your family does, too.

The Judds

Only a few years ago, Naomi and Wynonna Judd would routinely while away an evening at the table after dinner, harmonizing their own versions of their favorites by the Stanley Brothers, the Delmore Brothers, the Andrews Sisters and others. There wasn't much else to do for entertainment in Morrill, Kentucky, population 50. "We lived in a house with no telephone, no television, and no newspaper," remembers Naomi. "We just had a radio. On Saturday nights, we'd do the wash in our old Maytag wringer washer and listen to the Grand Ole Opry."

Today, the mother-daughter duo can hear their own records on the radio, including such #1 hits as "Mama, He's Crazy," "Why Not Me?" and "Girls' Night Out." They've earned a Grammy award for Best New Country Group, and their debut lp went gold.

The sudden fame has turned their world topsy-turvy. "I can't go to the supermarket anymore without 35- to 40-year-olds telling me how much they love my music," says 21-year-old Wynonna incredulously. Quite a shock for a girl who says she grew up "a typical Hollywood kid, eating Ding Dongs and watching 'The Brady Bunch' on TV." But that was before Naomi decided to leave Los Angeles and take her young daughters, Wynonna and Ashley (now a model), back to rural Kentucky, where she had grown up. After seven years in L.A., which had included a divorce and jobs as a model, manager of a health food store, secretary for the pop group The Fifth Dimension and girl Friday to a millionaire, Naomi thought it was time that the Judds returned to the basics. So they moved to Morrill (pronounced *moral*), where they rediscovered each other.

Naomi and Wynonna also discovered that they were good singing partners. In 1979, they moved to Nashville to try to make it as country singers. After four years – during which Naomi worked as a registered nurse in Franklin while Wynonna finished high school and then became a secretary – their efforts paid off.

It's been a big change for both mother and daughter. "At first I didn't know how I'd take to life on the road," says Naomi. "I've been cookin' and keepin' house and bein' a mom since I was about 17 years old. So I wondered, 'Am I gonna get the urge to run back into the kitchen of a restaurant one night and put on an apron, or get off the bus and mop and wax the freeway? But it hasn't happened yet."

Now Naomi saves her motherly instincts for the times when she's back at home. She has Judds band members visit often and likes to fix them meals of "pork chops and gravy and biscuits and rice and greasy beans and home-made iced tea." Meanwhile Wynonna, who has her own apartment and is a pretty fair cook herself, keeps practicing her guitar. She plays, she says, because "Mama wants to keep her fingernails."

Pee Wee King

Pee Wee King doesn't cook, never has (in the kitchen anyway). "I never had to," he says candidly and at his age (70), he's not likely to start learning now. "My wife, Lydia, has been cooking for me for 48 years and is still doing a great job." Before Lydia's cooking, Pee Wee feasted on his mother's food at home back in Milwaukee. He vividly recalls "the aroma of home-made bread and doughnuts baking, and all the good, hearty meals she cooked."

But good eating just couldn't keep Pee Wee at home. By the age of 20, he was playing his trademark accordion on "The Gene Autry Show," broadcast for radio out of Louisville. Two years later he was leading his own band, the Golden West Cowboys, on the Grand Ole Opry, where they remained popular regulars for the next ten years. Afterwards, he went on to tour extensively at home and abroad, and hosted his own radio and TV shows in Louisville, where he now makes his home. And to top it all, Pee Wee co-wrote (with band member Redd Stewart) one of the all-time classics of country and popular music, "The Tennessee Waltz."

Despite the hustle and the bustle of his career, Pee Wee managed to find time to eat hearty meals. "Back then on the road," he remembers, "I especially enjoyed a good breakfast of country ham, eggs, biscuits and gravy. (Today I use egg substitute.)"

When at home, he has always enjoyed meal time with family and friends. One particularly memorable meal took place when Roy Acuff came to dinner and asked for his dessert first. "As a boy," Pee Wee explains, "Roy was told he could do this if he then ate all of his dinner. I couldn't tell you what he ate, but I do remember the incident!"

As for Pee Wee, he eats his meals pretty much the regular way. "I like a well-balanced meal," he says. "I like fish, chicken and a steak now and then. Sometimes an all-vegetable plate satisfies me." He says he doesn't have a favorite food: "No real preference; I like most foods."

With the globe-trotting he's done, Pee Wee's had a chance to sample some exotic delicacies. He still remembers a dish he tried in Central America 40 years ago: "While we were touring as part of the Camel Caravan Grand Ole Opry unit entertaining U.S. troops in 1941-42, we played for the soldiers at the Taboga Outpost in Guatemala. After the show, the commandant invited the entire cast to eat at the main mess hall. The meal they served us *looked* like either chicken or fish. It was iguana."

None of the recipes Pee Wee has included here require any type of lizard as an ingredient.

Brenda Lee

Brenda Lee taught herself to cook and she likes what she's learned. "It gives me great satisfaction when it's edible," she jokes. Cooking for husband Ronnie Shacklett and daughters Julie and Jolie gives her even greater satisfaction. "My family always ate together when I was growing up and that tradition has carried over into my married life," she says.

Family meals were not easy to arrange when Brenda was young. Her father died when she was a little girl and consequently her mother had to work long hours in a cotton mill to make ends meet. Still, Brenda says, "I remember that no matter what we had, we had enough, and my mother always cooked three meals a day." (Brenda says her mother is still one of her favorite cooks; so is her mother-in-law.)

For her part, Brenda started singing for pay as soon as she could. By the age of six, she was performing with a television band on weekends. At age 11, she was a star, dubbed little Miss Dynamite by the press for her powerful, grown-up voice. That voice has sold nearly 90 million records with such hits as "I'm Sorry," "Rockin' Around the Christmas Tree," "Johnny One-Time" and "Tell Me What It's Like." Today, three decades later, she's still a popular entertainer.

Brenda lists her favorite foods as vegetables, chicken and beef stew. She says her favorite meal consists of fried chicken, fresh green beans, creamed potatoes, fried corn, collard or turnip greens, green onions, home-grown tomatoes, cornbread and iced tea. When she tours, she settles for omelettes, club sandwiches and vegetables ("when I can get them"). In a good restaurant, she prefers escargot, Caesar salad and veal picante. A couple of her favorite dining spots are Couser's Restaurant in Nashville and Broussard's in New Orleans.

The restaurant she visited once in Taiwan, though, didn't impress her. "It was a meal given to me by Chinese dignitaries," she recalls. "I had shark fin soup and a lot of other things that were questionable."

A better memory was certainly the dinner she had with Judy Garland. "The reason it was so memorable," says Brenda, "is that I was so awestruck by her. I can't remember what we ate!"

In the end, though, family has probably meant the most to Brenda. Even though she has performed in 36 countries and all over the U.S., she says that a dinner with her husband and daughters at a restaurant called Crickets in Boston in 1979 was her most memorable meal. And she always remembers holiday meals fondly, especially Christmas, because then, "all the people I love are together."

Veggies,
Breads
and Extras

RICKY SKAGGS' SWEET POTATO CASSEROLE

When buying fresh sweet potatoes, keep in mind that these do not store as well as ordinary potatoes. You can store them in a cool place for up to a week.

2	cups cooked and mashed sweet potatoes
1¼	cups sugar
½	cup margarine
1	cup milk
1	teaspoon vanilla
2	eggs, beaten well
1	teaspoon cinnamon
½	teaspoon nutmeg

Topping:

¾	cup margarine
½	cup chopped pecans
½	cup brown sugar, packed
¾	cup Rice Krispies cereal

Preheat oven to 400 degrees.

Thoroughly mix the first eight ingredients in a mixing bowl and place in a 10-inch square shallow baking dish. Bake 20 minutes.

Meanwhile, mix topping ingredients well. After baking potatoes 20 minutes, spread topping evenly on the cooked potatoes. Lower oven to 350 degrees and bake an additional 10 minutes.

Makes 10 to 12 servings.

REBA McENTIRE'S FAVORITE SWEET POTATO CASSEROLE

A Southern recipe popular for generations.

1	16-ounce can sweet potatoes, drained
¼	teaspoon salt
1	teaspoon vanilla
½	teaspoon cinnamon
⅓	cup sugar
¼	cup melted butter or margarine
2	eggs

Topping:

¼	cup melted butter or margarine
1	tablespoon flour
¾	cup brown sugar
½	cup chopped pecans

Preheat oven to 350 degrees.

In a large bowl, mash potatoes. Add remaining ingredients. Mix well. Pour into buttered 1-quart casserole dish. Mix topping ingredients thoroughly and sprinkle evenly over potato mixture. Bake for 30 minutes.

Makes 6 to 8 servings.

Editors Note: You may substitute 6 medium fresh sweet potatoes, boiled and peeled.

DEBORAH ALLEN'S HOLIDAY SWEET POTATOES

Great eating any day, but this recipe is particularly good with your Christmas and Thanksgiving feasts.

6	sweet potatoes, peeled, sliced and cooked
½	cup butter
1	teaspoon baking powder
1	teaspoon vanilla
1	teaspoon ground cinnamon
2	eggs, beaten
½	cup sugar
¾	cup buttermilk
¾	cup pecans, chopped

Topping:

⅓	cup melted butter
1	cup light brown sugar
½	cup flour
1	cup chopped pecans
	Marshmallows

Preheat oven to 350 degrees.

In a large bowl, mash sweet potatoes. Add butter and mix thoroughly. Add next 7 ingredients and stir. Place mixture in a buttered 2-quart casserole.

To make topping, melt butter in saucepan and mix in sugar, flour and pecans. Sprinkle marshmallows evenly on top of potatoes. Bake for 30 minutes. Top with marshmallows during last 10 minutes.

Makes 10 to 12 servings.

HELEN CORNELIUS' SWEET POTATO CASSEROLE

Sweet potatoes make a popular casserole and add an additional zip to a meal.

4½	cups cooked, mashed sweet potatoes
2	eggs, beaten
1	cup sugar
1	teaspoon vanilla
½-¾	cup butter

Topping:

1	cup brown sugar
1	cup chopped pecans
⅓	cup all-purpose flour
⅓	cup butter, melted

Preheat oven to 350 degrees.

Mix together sweet potatoes, eggs, sugar and vanilla. Melt butter. Add to other ingredients. Blend until smooth. Pour into lightly greased 1½-quart casserole. You may use more butter, according to your taste. I personally use about ¾ cup.

Topping: Mix ingredients together and spread over potato mixture. Bake for 30 minutes.

Makes 6 servings.

THE OAK RIDGE BOYS' SCALLOPED POTATOES

An easy recipe for an old-fashioned and very favorite American dish.

1	10¾-ounce can cream of celery soup, undiluted
½	cup milk
1	small onion, chopped
	Salt and pepper
4	cups potatoes, peeled and sliced

Preheat oven to 350 degrees.

Combine soup, milk and onion. Salt and pepper to taste. In a 9 by 9-inch baking dish, arrange one-half potatoes in a layer. Pour half soup mixture over potatoes; add second layer potatoes and pour remaining soup mix over them. Bake uncovered 1 hour or until potatoes are tender.

Makes 8 servings.

CONWAY TWITTY'S ORIGINAL SKILLET-FRIED POTATOES AND OKRA

Conway's wife, Mickey, developed this recipe because "I like okra and potatoes and I thought there must be a good way to put them together. Fixed this way, the okra is crisp, not slippery."

2	cups okra, sliced
	Salt and pepper
	Cornmeal to coat
4	large potatoes, sliced thinly
	Bacon drippings
1	onion, finely chopped (optional)

Salt and pepper okra to taste and coat well with cornmeal; set aside.

Heat bacon drippings in skillet to medium hot and add potatoes. Cover and slow fry until potatoes are soft, about 10 minutes. Toss occasionally. Remove cover. Turn heat to high and add okra and finely chopped onions, if desired. Fry until done, tossing occasionally to keep from sticking, about 5 minutes more.

Makes 4 servings.

B. J. THOMAS' CROCK POT MACARONI AND CHEESE

Use a crock pot when you need to prepare your food hours ahead of time and have it cook slowly.

2	cups evaporated milk
½	teaspoon paprika
1	teaspoon salt
2	tablespoons minced onion
2	cups cubed cheddar cheese
2	tablespoons butter
3-4	cups cooked macaroni
1	egg, beaten (optional)

Put all ingredients except macaroni and egg in crock pot. Stir well. Cover, cook 1 hour over low heat. Add macaroni. For a thicker sauce, add beaten egg just before adding macaroni. Cook 2 to 3 hours over low heat.

Makes 6 to 8 servings.

TOM T. HALL'S RIVER ROAD POTATOES

A real favorite of Tom T's. Tom found this recipe in an old cookbook and serves it regularly.

3   large cloves garlic, sliced
1   heaping teaspoon salt
½   teaspoon dry mustard
1   scant tablespoon sugar
1   tablespoon Worcestershire sauce
1   cup pure olive oil
½   cup tarragon vinegar
14-15 red potatoes
½   cup chopped parsley
½   cup chopped scallions

Combine garlic, salt, dry mustard, sugar, Worcestershire sauce, olive oil and vinegar in a bowl and let stand at least 1 hour, longer if a more pronounced garlic taste is desired. Strain mixture so there will be no garlic pieces in the sauce.

Meanwhile, place potatoes in large pot, cover with water and boil until done, about 15 to 20 minutes. Peel and cut in ½-inch chunks. Place in large bowl and sprinkle parsley and scallions over potatoes.

Pour garlic mixture over potatoes; stir well. Let stand at least 4 hours or all day, if possible. Stir every hour. Do not refrigerate.

Makes 6 to 8 servings.

Editors Note: Scallions are popularly known as green onions.

B. J. THOMAS' FRENCH FRIES

You may like to try leaving the potatoes unpeeled. The skin is delicious and packed with nutrients.

2   large potatoes (or as many as needed, depending on number to be served.)
    Vegetable shortening as needed
    Salt to taste

Peel potatoes and cut lengthwise into ¼-inch wide strips.

Bring shortening to very high temperature in 9 to 12-inch skillet or deep fryer.

Fry a few potato strips at a time in the hot shortening until crisp and golden. Remove and drain on paper towels. Sprinkle with salt and serve immediately.

Serves 1 per potato.

THE OAK RIDGE BOYS' "YORKSHIRE PUDDING" WITH BEEF CONSOMME

An original recipe by Joe Bonsall's wife, Mary, it's a favorite of Joe's.

½   cup butter
1   cup water
1   teaspoon salt
1   cup sifted all-purpose flour
4   fresh eggs
6-8   cups beef consomme

Preheat oven to 400 degrees.

In medium saucepan, heat butter and water over high heat. Stir until butter is melted; turn heat on low; add salt and flour both at once. Stir vigorously over low heat until mixture leaves sides of pan in a smooth, compact ball.

Immediately remove from heat; quickly add eggs, one at a time, beating with spoon until smooth after each addition. After last egg has been added, beat until mixture has satin-like sheen.

Drop mixture by tablespoonfuls, 3 inches apart on a greased cookie sheet. Shape each so that the center is in a point.

Bake 20 to 25 minutes or until golden.

Serve in bowls with hot beef consomme.

Makes 4 servings.

HELEN CORNELIUS' CORNBREAD DRESSING

A good side dish with chicken, turkey or pork. Wonderful for holiday dinners.

6   cups crumbled cornbread
⅓   cup chopped onion
1   cup chopped celery
2   tablespoons chopped parsley
1½   teaspoons salt
1   tablespoon poultry seasoning
1   teaspoon dried sage
½   teaspoon black pepper
     Turkey broth to moisten well
¼   cup butter, melted
3   eggs, beaten
1   4-ounce can mushroom pieces, drained

Preheat oven to 375 degrees.

In large bowl, mix all ingredients thoroughly. Pour into 9 by 13 by 2-inch baking pan and bake 1 hour. Serve with turkey gravy, or other gravy, if desired.

Makes 6 to 8 servings.

HANK WILLIAMS, JR.'S CAJUN RICE CASSEROLE

While Cajun cooking of Louisiana is similar to Creole cooking, Cajun foods are more robust and highly seasoned than the Creole cuisine of New Orleans.

½	pound bacon
1	large onion, chopped
1	teaspoon garlic salt
1	teaspoon onion salt
½	pound okra, trimmed and cut into small pieces
2	16-ounce can tomatoes with juice
1	10-ounce can Ro-Tel tomatoes and green chilies
3	tablespoons dried parsley flakes
	Salt and pepper
	Rice

Fry bacon in skillet and drain. Cool and crumble into small pieces. Saute onions in bacon grease until golden. Add garlic salt, onion salt, okra, tomatoes, Ro-Tel, parsley flakes, salt and pepper. Mix well. Simmer uncovered for 1½ hours.

Meanwhile, prepare servings of rice according to package directions. Serve cooked mixture over rice. Top with crumbled bacon.

Makes 4 to 6 servings.

THE STATLER BROTHERS' GREEN RICE

Some experts put the total varieties of rice recipes at more than 10,000. We recommend you add this one to your favorites.

1	large onion, finely chopped
1	rib celery, finely chopped
2	tablespoons butter
1	10¾-ounce can cream of celery soup, undiluted
1	10¾-ounce can cream of mushroom soup, undiluted
1	cup cooked rice
1	10-ounce package frozen broccoli, cooked and drained
1	8-ounce jar Cheez Whiz

Preheat oven to 325 degrees.

Saute onion and celery with butter in skillet.

In separate bowl, combine remaining ingredients. Mix thoroughly. Add onion and celery, and mix. Pour into 2-quart buttered baking dish. Bake for 25 minutes or until bubbling.

Makes 4 to 6 servings.

THE OAK RIDGE BOYS' MOUNTAIN MAN WILD RICE

The Oak Ridge Boys tell us that "Mountain men eat wild rice out of the skillet; city folks eat it out of a plate."

1½   cups wild rice, rinsed
3-4   cups water (more if needed)
1   onion, chopped
    Several wild dandelion greens, chopped
2   green peppers, chopped
    Bacon drippings
1   clove garlic, minced

Boil rice in water until almost done, about 30 minutes. Place onions, dandelion greens, and green peppers in skillet with bacon drippings. Stir a few minutes over medium heat; add rice. Stir. Cook for additional 5 minutes; add garlic.

Makes 4 servings.

GEORGE STRAIT'S SPANISH RICE

Delicious with George's recipe for Carne Guisada, Page 101.

1   cup raw rice
2   tablespoons vegetable shortening
1   small onion, chopped
½   bell pepper, chopped
1½   teaspoons salt
2   teaspoons chili powder
1   10-ounce can tomatoes, chopped
2   cups water

In a skillet, brown rice in shortening. Add the onion and bell pepper. Stir. Add salt, chili powder and tomatoes including juice. Add water. Cover and simmer 30 minutes, or until rice is tender and liquid is absorbed.

Makes 6 servings.

LEE GREENWOOD'S BROCCOLI AND RICE CASSEROLE

A super combination of foods. If you'd like to use fresh broccoli, we suggest steaming the flowerets from 1 head of broccoli before combining with the other ingredients.

2   10-ounce packages frozen chopped broccoli
1½   cups uncooked white rice
1   small onion, chopped
½   cup butter or margarine
1   8-ounce jar Cheez Whiz
1   10¾-ounce can cream of mushroom soup, undiluted
    Salt and pepper

Cook broccoli according to package directions and drain. Cook rice according to package directions.

Preheat oven to 350 degrees.

In a skillet, sauté onion in butter or margarine. Add broccoli, Cheez Whiz and mushroom soup; stir until cheese is melted. Add rice, plus salt and pepper to taste. Place in buttered 2-quart dish. Bake for 20 to 30 minutes or until bubbling.

Makes 8 servings.

EMMYLOU HARRIS' BROCCOLI NUT CASSEROLE

Emmylou served this at a potluck party held by Linda Ronstadt on the Fourth of July in Malibu. "They must have liked it," Emmylou says; "they ate it all up."

2   10-ounce packages frozen chopped broccoli
      Salt to taste
1   10¾-ounce can cream of mushroom soup, undiluted
1   cup mayonnaise
¾   cup chopped pecans
2   eggs, beaten
1   medium onion, chopped
1   cup shredded sharp cheddar cheese
½   cup dry bread crumbs

Preheat oven to 350 degrees.

Cook broccoli with salt according to package directions. Drain. Add soup, mayonnaise and chopped pecans. Mix well. Add eggs and onion. Pour into greased 1½-to 2-quart casserole. Sprinkle with cheese and top with bread crumbs. Bake for 30 minutes, or until bubbling.

Makes 6 servings.

REBA McENTIRE'S BROCCOLI CASSEROLE

This sidedish is quick to prepare. You may double the recipe and freeze half to enjoy later.

1   head fresh broccoli, chopped
1   10¾-ounce cream of mushroom soup, undiluted
1   8-ounce can sliced water chestnuts, drained
1   16-ounce jar Cheez Whiz
1   cup raw Minute Rice
1   cup cracker crumbs

Preheat oven to 375 degrees.

Steam broccoli just until crisp. Drain. Mix broccoli, soup, water chestnuts, Cheez Whiz and rice. Place in a greased 2-quart casserole. Top with cracker crumbs.

Bake about 20 to 30 minutes, or until bubbling.

Makes 6 to 8 servings.

RONNIE MILSAP'S STIR-FRY AMERICAN STYLE

Stir-frying is an Oriental cooking method that involves brief frying of foods in a minimum of oil over high heat. Stir-frying may be done either in a skillet or a wok. The results are crisp and tasty vegetables!

1½	cups thinly sliced carrot
1½	cups thinly sliced zucchini
½	cup chopped onion
⅓	cup Squeeze Parkay margarine
1	16-ounce can bean sprouts, drained
1	8-ounce can water chestnuts, drained and halved
1	4½-ounce jar whole mushrooms, drained
1	teaspoon salt
¾	cup Kraft grated parmesan cheese

Sauté carrots, zucchini and onion in margarine in large skillet until lightly browned, stirring occasionally. Add bean sprouts, water chestnuts, mushrooms and salt. Heat thoroughly, stirring constantly. Remove from heat, toss lightly with cheese before serving. Top with additional grated cheese, if desired.

Makes 6 servings.

DEBORAH ALLEN'S ASPARAGUS CASSEROLE

Asparagus has been a prized vegetable for over 2000 years. Cultivation requires a lot of special attention. Each spear is usually harvested individually with a special knife inserted into the soil.

1	tablespoon butter
	Crumbled Ritz crackers
2	10-ounce cans asparagus, drained and 1 tablespoon liquid reserved
2	hard-cooked eggs, sliced
1	10¾-ounce can golden mushroom soup, undiluted
½	teaspoon celery salt
	Salt and pepper
1⅓	cups shredded cheddar cheese

Preheat oven to 350 degrees.

Butter a 1-quart casserole and arrange some cracker crumbs on bottom. Place a layer of asparagus over crumbs. Cover with a layer of sliced eggs.

In a saucepan, heat soup. Add celery salt, salt and pepper to taste and liquid from asparagus. Pour half the soup over the eggs and sprinkle with ⅔ cup of cheese. Repeat layers. Top with more cracker crumbs. Bake until brown and bubbling, about 30 minutes.

Makes 6 servings.

Editors Note: When fresh asparagus is available you may want to use it. Substitute 1 pound fresh asparagus which has been blanched for 2 minutes in boiling water for the canned.

JERRY REED'S FRIED CORN

"When slicing kernels from the cob, be sure to scrape the ears well to get the 'milk' from the corn."

5	ears fresh corn
1	cup water
¼	cup margarine

Slice kernels off corn lengthwise. Scrape ears well. Place kernels in frying pan. Add water and margarine. Cover and simmer over medium-low heat until soft, about 15 minutes.

Makes 4 servings.

HELEN CORNELIUS' SOUTHERN-FRIED CORN

Corn has been grown in North and South America for more than 3000 years. And it obviously never has lost its popularity!

8	ears tender white corn
¼	cup bacon drippings
½	cup cream
½	cup water
	Salt and pepper to taste
1	tablespoon cornstarch
2	tablespoons water

Cut corn off cob and scrape cob to get milky juice. Heat bacon drippings in a skillet. Add corn, cream, water, and salt and pepper. Cook over low heat for about 10 minutes, stirring occasionally. Thicken with cornstarch dissolved in water, if necessary.

Makes 6 to 8 servings.

BILL ANDERSON'S CORN PUDDING

If you've had corn pudding before, you'll jump at the chance to make this one. If it is new to you, you may never want corn any other way!

2	tablespoons all-purpose flour
1	16½-ounce can white creamed corn
1	tablespoon sugar
1	cup milk
2	teaspoons salt
3	tablespoons butter, softened
3	eggs, beaten

Preheat oven to 325 degrees.

Mix flour and corn; add sugar, milk, salt and butter. Add eggs and mix well. Pour pudding into greased one-quart casserole. Place casserole in pan of hot water; bake 1 hour.

Makes 4 to 6 servings.

THE OAK RIDGE BOYS'
OLD TIME FAMILY CORN CASSEROLE

A fan of The Oak Ridge Boys sent them this recipe that has become a favorite of each.

1	ear corn for each person
	(Ingredients per ear of corn):
½	teaspoon dried onion flakes
¼	teaspoon salt
	Dash pepper
¼	teaspoon sugar
	Dash paprika
	Dash nutmeg
1	tablespoon butter
	Half-and-half cream
	Soda crackers, crushed
	Butter

Preheat oven to 350 degrees.

Butter casserole; cut corn off ears into the casserole. Scrape ear of corn to get all milk from it. Add onion flakes, salt, pepper, a little sugar, paprika and nutmeg. Dot corn with butter and mix lightly. Pour in cream to come up the side of the corn but not to cover it. Add soda crackers to cover top of corn and dot with with more butter. Bake for 30 minutes. Check after 20 minutes; be sure not to overcook or corn will be dry and tough.

Makes one serving per ear of corn.

THE OAK RIDGE BOYS' EGGPLANT PARMESAN

Excellent served as a side dish or as a main dish with tossed salad.

1	medium eggplant
2-3	eggs, beaten
1	cup Italian-seasoned bread crumbs
4	tablespoons Crisco shortening
1	quart Italian spaghetti sauce
1	pound mozzarella cheese, sliced thinly

Peel eggplant and slice thinly, ⅛-inch thick. Dip eggplant into eggs and then into bread crumbs; fry in pan with Crisco shortening, over medium heat until golden brown.

Preheat oven to 350 degrees.

In a 9 by 9 by 2-inch baking dish, spread thin layer spaghetti sauc on the bottom of dish; then arrange slices of eggplant over sauce; top with sliced mozzarella cheese and spaghetti sauce. Repeat until all eggplant is used. Finish with spaghetti sauce. Cover with foil and bake until cheese is melted and sauce is simmering at side of pan, about 35 to 40 minutes.

Makes 6 servings.

TAMMY WYNETTE'S EGGPLANT A LA TAMMY

Eggplant is an excellent absorber of spices and flavoring. Nutmeg is the secret ingredient that makes Tammy's eggplant special.

1	medium eggplant
	Flour
2	tablespoons butter
1	small onion, chopped
1	16-ounce can tomatoes
	pinch oregano
	Salt and pepper
3	tablespoons grated parmesan cheese
	Pinch nutmeg

Peel and dice eggplant and dredge in flour. Sauté eggplant in butter in a heavy skillet over medium heat, turning once. When browned slightly, remove to warm platter.

Preheat oven to 325 degrees.

Sauté onions in the same skillet until golden, but do not allow them to brown. Place eggplant and onions in a 1½-quart casserole. Add tomatoes, oregano, salt and pepper to taste. Mix carefully to blend ingredients and top with grated cheese. Sprinkle with nutmeg. Bake for 20 minutes until hot and bubbling and cheese has melted.

Makes 4 servings.

MINNIE PEARL'S ZUCCHINI SQUASH

Minnie says, "This is a great recipe, best suited to people who like Italian seasonings. If you prefer to use canned tomatoes instead of V-8 juice, it takes a little longer to cook. I use V-8 because of its different seasonings which add to the flavor of the zucchini. It's hard to say how much oregano to use. I like oregano, so I use a lot!"

4-5	green onions, chopped
2	tablespoons butter or margarine
3	large zucchini
	Salt and pepper
	Dried oregano
	V-8 juice
1	teaspoon brown sugar (optional)

In a heavy skillet or Dutch oven with lid, sauté green onions in butter until clear and tender.

Wash zucchini. Do not peel. Slice crossways. Place in skillet with sauteed onions. Sprinkle with salt, pepper and oregano to taste. Pour V-8 juice over zucchini until well-covered. Add brown sugar, if desired. Place lid on Dutch oven or skillet. Cook slowly over low heat until zucchini is very tender, about 10 minutes.

Makes 6 servings.

THE OAK RIDGE BOYS' BAKED ACORN SQUASH

Did you know that in China, squash is hollowed out and the vessels are carved with intricate patterns and used as party decorations?

1   medium acorn squash
1   medium apple, cored, diced
¼   cup raisins
3   tablespoons honey
     Cinnamon

Preheat oven to 350 degrees.

Cut squash in half lengthwise. Bake for 20 minutes. Remove seeds from squash.

In a separate bowl mix apples, raisins and honey; spoon into squash; sprinkle with cinnamon. Bake an additional 30 minutes in a covered pan with about ¼ inch water in bottom of the pan.

Makes 2 servings.

HELEN CORNELIUS' TURNIP GREENS AND HOG JOWL

Try this popular Southern vegetable with cornbread and the pot likker (juice) from the turnip greens. Helen says, "The pot likker is good for you!"

1   Hog jowl
1   quart water
1   hot red pepper pod, chopped
1   gallon turnip greens, cleaned
     Salt
     Pepper
     Baking soda

Place the hog jowl in a pot with water and red pepper. Let boil about 1 hour. Add cleaned turnip greens. Sprinkle with salt and pepper to taste. Add a pinch of soda. Stir well. Cook covered about 1 hour or until tender.

Makes 8 servings.

TANYA TUCKER'S FRIED GREEN "TOMATERS"

This recipe also works well with zucchini or yellow squash.

1   cup cracker crumbs
½   cup cornmeal
4   green tomatoes
1   egg, slightly beaten
1   cup oil for frying
     Salt and pepper to taste

Mix cracker crumbs and cornmeal. Slice tomatoes very thin. Dip slices in egg and dredge in cornmeal/cracker mixture (repeat if you like them extra-crispy.) Fry in very hot oil in deep skillet on both sides until golden. Season with salt and pepper to taste.

Makes 2 to 4 servings.

MICHAEL MARTIN MURPHEY'S CHILI RELLENOS CON QUESO

It's a good practice to carefully wash your hands after handling chilies. The juice can burn your eyes if you rub them with your hands accidentally.

Chili Rellenos

12	*long slender green chilies*
1	*pound cheddar cheese, shredded*
1½	*cups all-purpose flour*
1	*teaspoon salt*
	Pepper to taste
1	*cup milk*
1	*tablespoon cooking oil*
2	*eggs, slightly beaten*
	Vegetable oil for frying
1	*cup red chili sauce**

Chilies are best if long and tender. You must remove the tough outer skin of the chilies. Slit one side and remove the veins and seeds and place the chilies on a baking sheet 5 to 6 inches from broiler. Set oven to 450 degrees and leave the door open. Turn the chilies as they cook and let them blister (but not burn) evenly. Remove from the oven and plunge immediately into ice water. Peel stem downward and remove the rest of the seeds. Stuff chilies with cheese. Don't break the chilies.

Mix flour, salt and pepper. Add milk, cooking oil and eggs until a smooth batter is formed. Let stand covered for 2 hours. Then roll chilies in batter and fry in hot vegetable oil, turning until evenly brown. Drain. Serve with red chili sauce.*

*Red Chili Sauce

3	*tablespoons vegetable shortening*
2	*tablespoons all-purpose flour*
1	*clove garlic, minced*
½	*cup chili powder*
2	*cups water*
1	*teaspooon salt*

Get the best quality fresh chili powder you can find.

Melt shortening; blend in the flour and garlic and cook until mixed well. Add chili powder, water and salt and stir over moderate heat until completely combined and slightly thickened. Pour over Chili Rellenos and enjoy!

Makes 12 chili rellenos."

RICKY SKAGGS' PINTO BEANS

Ham hock or hog jowl is seasoned fat used in many Southern dishes. It can be bought in most grocery stores.

1½ cups dried pinto beans
    Water
1   ham hock or hog jowl
    Salt

Clean beans under fresh water, making sure that all discolored and bad beans are thrown out. In a saucepan, cover beans with water. Add ham hock or hog jowl and bring to a boil. Reduce heat and cook slowly for 4 to 5 hours, or until tender. Add salt to taste. Serve hot.

Makes 6 to 8 servings.

"MR. MONE'S" BEAN CASSEROLE

You'll notice that Ray Stevens' recipe titles refer to "Raymone" and "Mr. Mone". This is a clever alias for an unusual and funny man, Raymone "Mr. Mone" Stevens.

2   16-ounce cans cut green beans, drained
¾   cup Flav-O-Rich milk
1   10¾-ounce can cream of mushroom soup, undiluted
1   2.8-ounce can French-fried onions
    Salt and pepper to taste

Preheat oven to 350 degrees.

Mix all ingredients except ½ cup of French-fried onions; pour into 2-quart casserole. Bake 30 minutes. Remove from oven and spread remaining French fried onions on top of casserole; bake an additional 5 minutes.

Makes 4 to 6 servings.

Editors Note: Two pounds fresh green beans may be substituted for canned beans. Snip off ends, cut in one-inch pieces and cook over high heat, uncovered, for 7 to 8 minutes until tender, but not too soft. Drain. Then make the above recipe.

RAYMONE'S BEER BISCUITS

A new twist on an easy biscuit recipe! Serve hot with chili.

2   cups Bisquick baking mix
1   tablespoon sugar
8   ounces beer

Preheat oven to 350 degrees.

Mix Bisquick, sugar and beer. Spoon batter evenly into 12 greased muffin tins and bake 15 to 20 minutes or until brown.

Makes 12 biscuits.

THE OAK RIDGE BOYS' HOT BISCUITS

Nina Breland, bass player Don Breland's mother, says the secret of these biscuits is the lard: "I find they are much fluffier when you use lard. This is the one thing that Don really loves for breakfast with bacon and eggs. I cook mine in an iron skillet".

2   cups self-rising flour
1/4   teaspoon baking soda
1/3   cup lard
3/4   cup buttermilk

Preheat oven to 400 degrees.

Sift flour and soda together. Cut lard into flour mixture until particles are like fine crumbs.

Add buttermilk and stir with a fork until dough leaves side of bowl. Turn dough out onto lightly floured board or pastry sheet. Knead dough until smooth and press out to about 1/2-inch thickness.

Cut biscuits with floured 2-inch cutter. Place on greased baking sheet. Bake for 12 to 15 minutes.

Makes 12 to 14 2-inch biscuits.

KITTY WELLS' ANGEL BISCUITS

Kitty's biscuits are so light they will fly away like angels.

2   packages active dry yeast
1/2   cup warm water
5   cups all-purpose flour
1   teaspoon baking soda
2   teaspoons coarse salt
1   tablespoon baking powder
1   tablespoon sugar
3/4   cup vegetable shortening
2   cups buttermilk

Preheat oven to 400 degrees.

Dissolve yeast in 1/2 cup warm water. In a large bowl, sift dry ingredients together. Cut in shortening, then add yeast mixture and buttermilk. Mix with large spoon real good. This makes a real large bowl full.

You can pinch off each day just the amount you want to cook. Shape dough into small rolls and place on greased baking sheet. Bake 12 to 15 minutes.

Keep remainder of dough covered. It will keep a week to 10 days in the refrigerator.

Makes a few dozen biscuits depending on size.

TANYA TUCKER'S BRAIDED BREAD

A very pretty-looking yeast bread.
Try one loaf with sesame seeds
and one with poppy seeds.

2   packages active dry yeast
2½ cups warm water
1   tablespoon salt
7-8 cups all-purpose flour
    Sesame seeds or poppy seeds

Dissolve yeast in ½ cup warm water. Mix salt and 4 cups flour, add 2 remaining cups water and mix until smooth. Add dissolved yeast and remaining flour to make a stiff dough. Turn out on floured board, add more flour if needed and knead 10 to 15 minutes.

Place in a greased bowl, cover with a damp cloth and let rise till double in size (about 1½ hours.) Punch down and let rise covered, till double again (about 45 minutes.) Divide dough in two pieces. Let rest 10 minutes.

Preheat oven to 375 degrees.

Divide each piece into three balls and roll each ball into 16-inch strips. Braid 3 strips to make a loaf. Sprinkle with sesame seeds or poppy seeds, place loaves on greased baking sheet, cover and let rise about ½ hour. Bake 30 to 40 minutes, or until golden brown.

Makes 2 loaves.

THE STATLER BROTHERS' EASY FRENCH BREAD

An easy recipe because the dough is made and kneaded in a food processor.

1½ packages active dry yeast
1½ cups warm water
3½ cups all-purpose flour
2   teaspoons salt
1   teaspoon sugar

In a glass measuring cup, dissolve yeast in ½ cup water and set aside for 5 minutes.

Mix flour, salt and sugar in food processor fitted with steel blade and add yeast mixture. Process about 20 seconds. Gradually add remaining 1 cup water until dough forms a ball. (It may not be necessary to use all of the water.)

Remove dough and roll on floured board or pastry cloth. Divide dough into two parts and slightly twist. Place loaves on a greased baking sheet, cover with a damp cloth and let rise until double in size, about one hour.

Preheat oven to 450 degrees when loaves are almost doubled in size. Bake for 10 to 15 minutes or until golden brown. (Place pan of water in oven under bread during baking.)

Makes 2 loaves.

Editors Note: Misting loaves of French Bread while baking helps make a crisp crust.

MINNIE PEARL'S ROLLS

If you're baking for a crowd, this is the bread recipe for you!

1	package active dry yeast or 1 cake compressed yeast
½	teaspoon sugar
½	cup warm water
½	cup vegetable shortening
½	cup sugar
1	egg, beaten
1	teaspoon salt
2	cups warm water
8-9	cups sifted, all-purpose flour

Dissolve yeast and ½ teaspoon sugar in ½ cup warm water.

In separate bowl, cream shortening and sugar. Add egg, salt and warm water. Mix in 2 cups flour. Add yeast mixture. Mix in remaining flour a little at a time to form a thick dough that can be kneaded. Turn out on a floured cloth or board. Let rest 10 minutes.

Preheat oven to 400 degrees.

Knead dough until smooth and satiny about 5 to 10 minutes. Place dough in greased bowl. Turn to grease top. Cover with cloth and let rise in a warm place until double in bulk. Punch down. Turn out on floured board or cloth. Knead until smooth, about 5 minutes. Roll out. Shape into small rolls. Place on greased baking sheet. Bake for 12 to 14 minutes or until done.

Makes about 6 dozen rolls.

CONWAY TWITTY'S "DUDE'S CORNBREAD"

Conway tells us that Dude was a cook at Moon Lake Resort who made the best cornbread ever. She let the Twittys in on her secret: Dude cooked her cornbread in an old oven that had no temperature controls. She would heat the oven as hot as it would go, then rely on instinct. Naturally, for Dude it came out perfectly every time!

2	tablespoons Wesson oil
1	cup cornmeal
1	tablespoon all-purpose flour
1	teaspoon sugar
½	teaspoon baking soda
1	cup buttermilk
½	teaspoon salt
½	cup water

Preheat oven to 450 degrees.

Grease and heat an 8-inch skillet with Wesson oil.

Stir together remaining ingredients, mixing just to combine. Pour batter into hot, greased skillet. Bake for 20 minutes or until golden.

Makes 4 servings.

DOLLY PARTON'S CORN PONE

"Pones," cornmeal cakes shaped like ovals, originated with the Algonquin Indians.

2	cups cornmeal
1	teaspoon salt
2	teaspoons all-purpose flour
2	teaspoons bacon grease
	Milk (use enough to make a stiff batter), about 1 cup

Mix all ingredients together, then form pones by hand and put on a greased baking sheet. Bake 12 to 15 minutes at 425 degrees.

Makes about 1½ dozen, depending on size.

BRENDA LEE'S SOUTHERN SPOON BREAD

Brenda suggests serving this Southern favorite with heaps of butter.

2	cups milk
4	egg yolks
1	cup white cornmeal
¼	cup butter or margarine, softened
1	tablespoon sugar
½	teaspoon salt
4	egg whites

Preheat oven to 375 degrees.

In top of double boiler over simmering water, scald milk. Meanwhile, beat egg yolks until thick and lemon-colored; set aside. When milk is scalded, very gradually add cornmeal, stirring constantly. Stir until mixture thickens and becomes smooth.

Remove top of double boiler from simmering water. Quickly and thoroughly blend mixture into the beaten egg yolks. Add butter, sugar and salt; blend thoroughly.

In separate mixing bowl, using clean beaters, beat egg whites until rounded peaks are formed. Spread egg yolk and cornmeal mixture over beaten egg whites and gently fold together. Turn into well-greased 2-quart casserole.

Bake for 35 to 40 minutes, or until a wooden pick or cake tester comes out clean when inserted into center.

Makes 6 to 8 servings.

RICKY SKAGGS' FRIED CORNBREAD

For variety, Ricky suggests omitting the cheese in this recipe and substituting one-half pound of bulk pork sausage, browned and drained. Serve with syrup.

1	cup cornmeal
⅔	cup all-purpose flour
1½	teaspoons baking powder
½	teaspoon salt
¾	cup milk
¼	cup margarine, melted
1	egg, beaten
1	cup shredded sharp cheddar cheese

Combine cornmeal, flour, baking powder and salt. In separate bowl, mix milk, margarine and egg. Add to dry ingredients, mixing just until moistened. Stir in cheese.

For each serving, spoon approximately ¼ cup mixture onto hot, lightly greased griddle or skillet; flatten batter slightly. Cook until lightly browned on both sides.

Serve warm with additional margarine. If batter becomes too thick, add small amount of milk.

Makes 6 to 8 servings.

REBA McENTIRE'S MEXICAN CORNBREAD

A casserole that is a fantastic concoction and which makes a nice light meal with a salad.

1	medium onion, diced
2	tablespoons butter
1	pound ground beef
1	6½-ounce package Mexican cornbread mix
1	8½-ounce package Jiffy cornbread mix
1	9-ounce jar Mexican jalapeno cheese dip
1	16-ounce can whole kernel corn, drained

Preheat oven to 375 degrees.

In skillet, brown diced onions in butter. Add ground beef to onions and brown. Remove from heat. Drain and set aside.

In bowl, mix cornbread according to package directions and combine batters. Grease or spray with vegetable cooking spray a 9 by 13 by 2-inch baking pan. Put a thin layer of cornbread mixture on bottom of pan. Next, add meat and onion mixture, then add cheese dip and corn. Pour remaining cornbread mixture on top.

Bake for about 30 mintues, or until golden brown.

Makes 6 to 8 servings.

CONWAY TWITTY'S HUSH PUPPIES

Mickey learned to make hush puppies for husband Conway after she discovered his liking for fresh fish. She discovered this early in their marriage when she found fresh fish, compliments of Conway, swimming in her bathtub!

3	cups yellow cornmeal
2	teaspoons baking powder
1½	teaspoons salt
1½	cups milk
½	cup water
1	egg, beaten
1	onion, finely chopped
	Bacon drippings for frying

Stir together cornmeal, baking powder and salt. Add milk, water, egg and onion. Mix well.

Heat 1 inch bacon drippings in a skillet over medium heat until very hot, but not smoking. Drop tablespoons of the batter into the fat and fry turning occasionally until crisp and golden, about 2 minutes. Lift from skillet with a slotted spoon and drain on paper towels.

Makes 6 servings.

GEORGE STRAIT'S FLOUR TORTILLAS

Place a tablespoon guacamole salad, shredded cheese or chili in center of each tortilla and either roll up or fold in half.

4	cups all-purpose flour
1	teaspoon baking powder
1	teaspoon salt
	Pinch of sugar
3-4	tablespoons vegetable shortening
	Hot water
	Vegetable oil

Combine dry ingredients in a large mixing bowl. Cut in shortening. Add just enough hot water to make a wet dough (not too light and not too stiff). Shape dough into small meatball-size rolls. On a floured surface roll the balls out very thin (about ⅛-inch thick). Cook in hot skillet, brushed with vegetable oil turning to brown both sides.

Makes 4 to 6 servings.

EDDY RAVEN'S CHEWY BREAD

Eddy's bread makes a wonderful breakfast treat but is also good with dinner.

1	pound light brown sugar
½	cup butter or margarine, softened
3	eggs
2	cups self-rising flour
1	teaspoon vanilla
1	cup chopped pecans

Preheat oven to 350 degrees.

In saucepan, melt brown sugar and butter. Turn into mixing bowl. Add eggs, one at a time, stirring well after each. Add flour. Blend well. Add vanilla and pecans. Stir thoroughly. Pour batter into a greased 13 by 9 by 2-inch baking pan. Bake for 30 minutes. Cool. Cut into squares.

Makes 12 squares.

THE OAK RIDGE BOYS' BANANA NUT BREAD

To make gift rounds of Banana Bread save your soup tin cans, wash thoroughly and use as baking pans for small rounds of the bread. These are pretty wrapped in clear cellophane and tied with a bright ribbon for gifts.

1	cup sugar
¼	cup melted butter
1	egg, slightly beaten
3	mashed bananas
1½	cups sifted all-purpose flour
1	teaspoon salt
1	cup chopped nuts (pecans or walnuts)

Preheat oven to 350 degrees.

Combine sugar and butter; add egg. Add bananas. Combine flour and salt and add to sugar and egg mixture. Stir in nuts.

Pour into greased all-floured 5 by 9-inch loaf pan. Bake for 45 to 60 minutes.

Makes 1 large or 2 small loaves. However, baking time will be shorter with smaller loaves.

THE WHITES' APPLE BUTTER

Cheryl White gave pints of apple butter one Christmas as gifts and says she "received many compliments" for her efforts.

2	dozen apples (6 pounds)
2	quarts apple cider
3	cups sugar
1½	teaspoons ground cinnamon
½	teaspoon ground cloves

Core and slice apples (don't peel). Place apples and cider in a large kettle and cook until tender. Press apples through a sieve or food mill (be aware the peels may be difficult to press, just throw them out). This makes approximately 5 quarts of pulp.

Cook pulp over low heat until thick enough to "round up" on a spoon, stirring now and then to prevent sticking. Add sugar and spices and cook over low heat for 1 hour or until thick. Pour into hot, sterilized jars and seal properly.

Makes 8 to 10 pints.

Editors note: McIntosh or Rome Beauties are excellent varieties to use for this recipe. However any cooking apple may be used.

BRENDA LEE'S SWEET GREEN TOMATO PICKLES

Brenda makes her spice bag for this recipe by cutting a double thickness of cheesecloth into a 5-inch square. She then places the spices in the center of the cheesecloth and ties the ends together.

7 pounds green tomatoes
1 cup coarse salt
1 quart cider vinegar
2 cups sugar
4 teaspoons whole cloves
3 2 inch cinnamon sticks, broken
4 teaspoons whole allspice

Rinse tomatoes. Remove stems and slice. Place one half of the tomatoes in a large bowl. Add ½ cup of the salt. Repeat with remaining tomatoes and salt. Cover and let set overnight.

The following day, drain tomatoes, discarding liquid. In large kettle, mix vinegar and sugar. Heat to boiling, stirring until sugar is dissolved.

Place spices together in a spice bag and tie. Add to kettle along with tomatoes. Simmer 10 minutes over medium heat.

Fill 4 1-pint sterilized jars with pickles and seal jars. Process 10 minutes in a boiling water bath. Remove. Label jars with canning date, contents and store in a cool dry place.

Makes about 4 pints.

Editors Note: To assemble a boiling water bath fill a large kettle with enough water to cover jars by 1 inch. Heat to boiling. Carefully place sealed jars in kettle and cover. Start timing when water comes back to a boil.

MINNIE PEARL'S STUFFED PICKLES

This is an attractive and tasty addition to an appetizer tray.

2 very large dill pickles
1 5½-ounce jar any cheese spread

Cut ends from pickles. Using apple corer, scoop out seedy pulp. Fill pickles with cheese spread. Chill several hours. Cut in ¼-inch slices.

Makes 2 to 4 dozen slices.

T. G. SHEPPARD'S CHEESE GRITS

A spicy twist on plain grits that has become as popular in the South as plain grits.

1	cup uncooked grits
4	cups water
1	tablespoon salt
½	cup butter, cut up
1	6-ounce roll garlic cheese spread, cut up (about 1 cup)
½	pound sharp cheddar cheese, shredded
2	tablespoons Worcestershire sauce
	Paprika

In saucepan, cook grits in water with salt until done, according to package directions.

Preheat oven to 350 degrees.

Add butter, cheeses, and Worcestershire sauce to grits. Stir until butter and cheeses are melted. Pour into greased 1½- to 2-quart casserole dish. Sprinkle with paprika. Bake for 15 to 20 minutes, or until bubbling.

Makes 8 servings.

TAMMY WYNETTE'S GARLIC CHEESE GRITS

Grits are ground dried corn and, especially in the South, are eaten in a variety of ways. This recipe adds ingredients that give it an extra spark.

1	cup uncooked grits
4½	cups water
1	teaspoon salt
½	cup butter
1	6-ounce roll garlic cheese spread
2	eggs
½	cup milk
1	cup cornflakes, buttered (melted butter drizzled over cornflakes)

Cook grits with water and salt until thick and water is absorbed. Cool 15 minutes.

Preheat oven to 350 degrees. Melt butter and ¾ of the cheese stick; stir into the grits.

In a separate bowl, beat eggs with milk and stir into grits. Pour grits into greased 1½-quart baking dish and top with remaining cheese, crumbled, and the cornflakes. Bake for 25 to 30 minutes, or until bubbling.

Makes 6 servings.

HANK WILLIAMS, JR.'S SAUSAGE TREATS

These sausage balls freeze well wrapped tightly or placed in an air-tight container. When ready to use simply thaw, warm and serve.

1   pound sausage
¾   cup Bisquick baking mix
2   cups shredded cheddar cheese
1   tablespoon dried parsley flakes

Preheat oven to 400 degrees.

In a skillet, brown and drain sausage. Combine sausage and remaining ingredients in a large bowl. Mix well. Form mixture into small balls and place on lightly-greased baking sheet. Bake for 10 to 15 minutes or until golden brown.

Makes 1½ to 2 dozen, depending on size.

THE STATLER BROTHERS' SAUSAGE 'N' CHEESE BRUNCH TREATS

As the name suggests, great for brunch. Also a nice hors d'oeuvre or even a breakfast treat.

½   pound bulk pork sausage
1¼   cups Bisquick baking mix
¼   cup butter or margarine, softened
2   tablespoons boiling water
½   cup half-and-half cream
1   egg
2   tablespoons thinly-sliced green onions
¼   teaspoon salt
½   cup shredded Swiss cheese

Preheat oven to 375 degrees.

Generously grease 12 muffin cups, 2½ by 1¼ inches. Brown sausage and drain. In a bowl, mix Bisquick and butter. Add boiling water; stir vigorously until soft dough forms. Press one level tablespoon dough on bottom and up side of each muffin cup. Divide sausage evenly among cups.

Beat together half-and-half and egg; stir in onions and salt. Spoon equal amount into each cup; sprinkle cheese over top of each cup.

Bake until edges are golden brown and centers are set, about 25 minutes. Unused tarts may be refrigerated for future use.

Makes 12 tarts.

ALABAMA'S DELI DOGS

Mark Herndon enjoys motorcycling and flying, so these quick-to-fix Deli Dogs fit into his busy schedule!

4   jumbo Bryan hot dogs with cheese
4   slices white or whole wheat bread
      Mayonnaise and Dijon-style mustard
4   slices Swiss cheese

Boil hot dogs for 6 minutes. Spread mayonnaise and mustard on bread slices and top with a slice of cheese. Remove hot dogs from water and place them on bread slices. Fold over bread and enjoy. Makes 2 servings.

MICHAEL MARTIN MURPHEY'S AVOCADO PARTY DIP

A favorite of Michael's, this party dip was given to him by Diane Roller, Michael's assistant and president of his fan club!

3   ripe avocados, peeled, pit removed
1   16-ounce carton sour cream
1   8-ounce jar picante sauce (I like Pace brand)
1   pound cheddar cheese, shredded
2   cups chopped green onion tops
      Corn chips

Mash avocados in bottom of square, 8" x 8" glass baking dish. Cover with sour cream. Pour picante sauce evenly over sour cream, then cover with layer of shredded cheese. Top with chopped green onions and serve with corn chips.

(The picante sauce by Pace comes in hot, medium and mild, so pick to taste.)

Makes 6 to 8 appetizer servings.

RAY STEVENS' GREEN GODDESS DIP

Ray's rich and spicy dip is good served with crackers, chips or fresh vegetables cut into bite-size pieces.

2   3-ounce packages cream cheese, softened
1   cup mayonnaise
1   cup Flav-O-Rich sour cream
2   tablespoons lemon juice
4   tablespoons tarragon vinegar
1   scant tablespoon garlic salt
½   cup chopped green onions, using more tops than bottoms
⅔   cup chopped fresh parsley

Mix all ingredients until smooth.

Makes approximately 3½ cups.

BOBBY BARE'S MEXICAN FIESTA DIP

Serve this at your next party. Depending on the size of your get-together, you may want to double, or even triple, Bobby's recipe.

1	16-ounce can refried beans
1	1¼-ounce package dry taco seasoning mix
1	5-ounce jar green olives, drained and sliced
1	3¼-ounce can seedless black olives, drained and sliced
1	green pepper, diced
2-3	green onions, diced
2	4-ounce containers Kraft avocado dip (or homemade avocado dip)
1½	cup shredded cheddar cheese
1	11-ounce package taco chips

Combine refried beans with taco mix. Set aside. In a separate bowl combine olives, pepper and onions. Set aside.

On a large platter, layer in the following order refried bean mix, avocado dip, olives, pepper and green onion mix. Top generously with cheese. Serve with taco chips.

Makes 6 to 8 servings.

THE STATLER BROTHERS' CHEESE BALL

We suggest a sharp cheddar cheese for the shredded cheese in this popular recipe.

2	cups shredded cheese
1	3-ounce package cream cheese
	Dash garlic salt
3-5	dashes celery salt, or to taste
2	tablespoons finely grated onion
½	teaspoon Worcestershire sauce
3	tablespoons mayonnaise
¼	cup chopped green olives

In mixing bowl, combine all ingredients. Mix thoroughly. Form into a ball. Wrap tightly in plastic wrap and chill. Serve with crackers.

Makes 1 cheese ball.

PEE WEE KING'S PARTY CHEESE BALL

These cheese balls freeze well. Make sure to wrap them tightly with plastic wrap before freezing.

3	16-ounce packages cream cheese, softened
1	5-ounce jar Kraft Old English Cheese Spread
1	2-to 3-ounce wedge blue cheese
	Dash garlic powder
1	teaspoon Worcestershire sauce
1	teaspoon Lawry's seasoning salt
1	cup chopped pecans or chopped parsley

Combine all ingredients except pecans or parsley. Mix well. Form into 1 large or 2 small balls. Roll in nuts or parsley. Serve with your favorite crackers.

Makes 1 large or 2 small cheese balls.

Barbara Mandrell

Barbara Mandrell speaks for a lot of us when she says, "I love to cook but I hate to clean up afterwards." She's just as candid when she names her favorite cook: herself. She prefers her own cooking "because I know what I like and I can cook to suit my own taste. I like just about everything except anchovies, liver, and escargot," Barbara says. "My favorite meal is whatever I'm currently eating — just as my favorite record is always my latest release."

"Holiday meals are very special," she says, "and are the only times that I fix turkey and all the trimmings." Christmas is extra-special for Barbara because it's also her birthday: "I've been performing ever since I was a little girl, but Christmas was always a time to stop and spend some time with family and friends. Even though it was my birthday, and I probably could have gotten out of it if I'd wanted to, I always threw myself into the middle of food preparation. Even today, when my schedule allows, I consider it a treat when I'm able to cook."

Barbara has been known for going all-out all her life. Before she could read books, her mother had taught her to read music and play the accordion. By the time she was a teenager, she also could play steel guitar, bass, banjo and saxophone. Soon she was performing with her family. She took a brief vacation from show business when she married Ken Dudney, but she was soon back onstage, with Ken's support. In the '70s and '80s she had numerous hits, including "Midnight Oil," "Sleeping Single in a Double Bed" and "I Was Country When Country Wasn't Cool." For two seasons, she starred with her sisters in her own network TV variety show, and she was the first artist to twice win the CMA's Entertainer of the Year award (1980-81).

In the midst of her busy career, Barbara has somehow managed to remain a devoted wife to Ken and mother to son Matthew, daughter Jaime, and her new baby son, Nathaniel. She had a good role model in her own mother, who took care of a touring musical family during Barbara's formative years. "My mother has always been a very good cook," Barbara says, "and our family meals were always plentiful and special. We always had big meals with lots of company. That hasn't changed much today. We still have family dinner when we are all in town, and there is usually company over eating with us." On tour Barbara tries to take along a little of her life at home. When Matthew and Jaime were tots, she took them on the road with her, just as she is now doing with her baby son, Nathaniel. Meals are always as home-cooked as they can get on a rolling bus.

Of all the meals Barbara's ever had, a few stand out distinctly in her mind. The worst was the first meal she cooked as Mrs. Ken Dudney. The best was probably the time she had dinner with the President, even though she was so thrilled by the company that she can't remember what she ate. But perhaps the most memorable meal of all, she says, was her first solid meal in the hospital after the September 11, 1984, automobile wreck that nearly proved fatal to Barbara and her children. Now that she's recovered, Barbara's ready to take on the world again.

Barbara says she included the recipes in this cookbook, "because of the variety and because they are some fairly easy but delicious items to eat. I hope everyone likes them."

Reba McEntire likes to cook almost as much as she likes to sing or eat. "Cooking is something I very seldom get to do," says the perky daughter of a former champion steer roper, "because I'm on the road so much. It's fun for me to be able to go into the kitchen and cook up a meal. I'm my favorite cook, and I always cook my favorite stuff: baked beans, cole slaw, red beans, Mexican cornbread, fried potatoes — nothing too fattening!"

Reba learned how to cook — and how to sing and ride horses — on the family ranch in southeastern Oklahoma, where she was the third of four children. "Daddy had a lot of cattle spread out over 8000 acres. We'd get up before the sun, eat breakfast, ride the horses in the dark and herd the cattle back toward the house. Coming in at night, it would be so dark that all you could see were the sparks from the horses' shoes hitting the rocks. We'd sing just to keep ourselves awake."

Reba's singing on the ranch and on the family's summer trips on the rodeo circuit paid off. She blossomed into the CMA Female Vocalist of the Year for 1984 and 1985 with such hits as "Can't Even Get The Blues," "You're the First Time I've Ever Thought About Leaving, "How Blue" and "Somebody Should Leave." For her powerful, bluesy country sound, she has been touted as Patsy Cline and Loretta Lynn rolled into one.

Reba is on the road often these days, where she says she eats "a wide variety — from deli trays to the nice restaurants in the various cities we play in." For all the touring, though, she's still partial to food close to home. Her favorite local restaurant remains The Burger Shack in Stringtown, Oklahoma ("both locations"). Her most memorable meal took place when her husband, steer wrestling champion Charlie Battles, took her out to celebrate her thirtieth birthday at the Isle of Capri restaurant, located in Krebs, Oklahoma.

When not touring the country or recording in Nashville, Reba is home on a 215-acre ranch near Stringtown with Charlie. "You know, when I get home," she says, "we don't talk music. Momma and Daddy come up and we talk cattle business. You get away from it (the music business) and you realize that you're not the only one in this world or the most important thing."

To Reba, family is important. She remembers that despite the long hours of work on the ranch when she was growing up, her folks always had family dinner. "We all sat down together," she says, "except Pake, my older brother, who was always late coming in from the roping pen. Now we're on the road so much, we don't get to sit down together very often."

That's one reason why Thanksgiving is such a special time for Reba. "Thanksgiving is my favorite holiday meal for a couple of reasons. First of all our family (about 50 people) get together, and during the prayer, each person contributes to the prayer, saying what they are most thankful for. Also, we have pumpkin pie at Thanksgiving, and I *love* pumpkin pie."

Reba McEntire

Ronnie Milsap

Ronnie Milsap loves to eat. "It's amazing," he once told *People* magazine, "that I can be so disciplined in other ways and undisciplined in eating."

But, says Ronnie, "my biggest indulgence is my family — my wife, Joyce, and my son, Todd. Since I'm on tour a lot, every minute with them is really special." So, whenever Ronnie is about to tour without his family, they sit down to a meal that's become a Milsap family tradition — home-made tacos. "My second biggest indulgence," adds Ronnie, "is chocolate, and that shows in my waistline." To make up for his sweet tooth, he jogs regularly with members of his band.

In recent years, he's also been careful to eat nutritious foods. He now stocks his tour bus with fresh fruits, vegetables and nuts. Fresh food, he says, gives him the stamina to keep up a hectic schedule. The CMA Male Vocalist of the Year for 1974, 1976 and 1977 is constantly in demand to sing such soulful hits as "Pure Love," "There's No Gettin' Over Me," "Stranger in My House" and "She Keeps the Home Fires Burning."

Ronnie grew up in the hill country of Robbinsville, North Carolina, where he couldn't indulge himself in much of anything except his love of music. Born with congenital glaucoma which left him blind, Ronnie was turned over to his grandparents in his first year of life. Very soon, he demonstrated his yearning to make music. Ronnie's step-grandfather, Homer Frisby, remembers (in an interview with journalist Jerry Bledsoe): "When he was just a little thing, he used to get up under the house. I had two ol' metal barrels under there. He'd get up under there, get a stick of stove wood in each hand, and sing as loud as he could, a-beatin' on them barrels."

Ronnie's grandparents knew that education was the best thing for their grandson, so they arranged for him to go away to the Morehouse School for the blind. There he learned to play violin, woodwinds, guitar and his main instrument, keyboards. More importantly, he learned self-reliance and found his true calling. Later, during junior college, he found his wife, Joyce. Several years of unnoticed records and club dates in Georgia, New York and Memphis followed before Ronnie tried Nashville and became an "overnight sensation" in 1973.

Today, Ronnie's success at doing what he enjoys most, making music, has provided the Milsaps with a fine seven-and-a-half-acre home in Nashville, where the Milsaps grow many of their own vegetables. They use them in a couple of Ronnie's favorite recipes, which he's included in this cookbook.

Michael Martin Murphey

Michael Martin Murphey takes the food he eats seriously, but he knows how to enjoy it, too. "Today I eat for health," he says. "I love whole grains and vegetables. We eat from our garden here in Taos, New Mexico. We buy natural foods from a local co-op and farmers market. On tour, too, I get as much vegetarian, healthy-style food as possible, and I avoid fried foods. Fish and chicken fill in when vegetarian is unavailable."

Michael wasn't reared in a vegetarian family. His diet is something he's worked to change. Still, he has fond memories of the traditional meals he had as a youngster in Oak Cliff, Texas. "My mother always made great potato salad for our church picnics," he says. "And my dad did great barbecued steaks. I don't eat red meat anymore, but it was great when I did. I still love Mom's potato salad. She is an excellent cook and she has been concerned about nutrition as long as I can remember. We had good, basic meals with roast beef, potatoes, lots of vegetables and rolls on Sundays."

Even though Michael no longer feels the same as his dad about steaks, they always shared the same opinion about sweets. "My dad didn't care much for desserts or chocolate," says Michael. "I generally don't care for holiday meals because there's always too much and a lot of desserts are served. I don't care for sweets very much at all. I will make two exceptions: bananas foster and pumpkin pie."

In 1983, Michael was named Best New Male Vocalist by the Academy of Country Music. It was an unusual honor, especially since Michael had already recorded ten albums before he received the award. His musical career actually stretches back to the '60s at UCLA. There, he studied literature, venturing into clubs at night to play alongside such unknowns as Jackson Browne and Linda Ronstadt. In 1970, he moved back to Austin and became a popular fixture on the local club circuit. Five years later, Michael had his first big hit, "Wildfire," followed by "Carolina in the Pines." Recently he has come back with such hits as "What's Forever For" and "What She Wants."

None of the ebb and flow of stardom seems to have disturbed him much. "I guess my lifestyle has always been a bit off the beaten path," he observes. "Even now when many of my current releases have been Top Ten hits, I don't live in New York, Los Angeles or Nashville. My family (wife Mary and three children) and I live in Taos, close to the land and the incredible New Mexico environment." And he still prefers a solid meal of chile rellenos with rice and beans to just about anything. He also likes Italian food and sushi. Michael's most cherished meal was at his parent's fortieth wedding anniversary. And vegetarian or not, his worst meal was a spinach salad served to him by a friend . . . who forgot to wash the spinach.

The best meals of all, though, can be very simple, like the dinner he had with a man at a Hopi Indian reservation in Arizona. "His name was Llama Anagakira Govinda," says Michael. "It was a simple meal of nuts, grains, seeds, and steamed vegetables. It was his humor and his stories that made the meal special."

The Oak Ridge Boys

All for one and one for all. Onstage or off, The Oak Ridge Boys are a team. Each member of the quartet has a role. When they're singing, Duane Allen is usually the lead, Joe Bonsall, the tenor (and stage spokesman), William Lee Golden, the baritone and Richard Sterban, the bass. When they're not singing, they're still a team. Richard handles interviews and publicity; William Lee plans the Oaks' promotional moves; Joe organizes the charity functions; and Duane heads the business end of The Oak Ridge Boys' multimillion-dollar corporation.

Teamwork has paid off: a gold record for "Bobbie Sue," a platinum record for "Elvira" and packed houses wherever they tour. "We all realize that the group concept is what's responsible for the success we've enjoyed," explains Richard. "It's kind of like the seasons," adds William Lee. "There are four Oaks; there are four seasons. Each is allowed to be himself."

True, and when it comes to eating, it's every Oak for himself. Joe, who grew up in Philadelphia, enjoys dining out, especially on Italian food. "For the most part," he confides, "I am not a cook. But I love to eat." On tour, he's usually content with cheeseburgers and pizza. In Nashville, he likes the haute cuisine at Arthur's. In fact, Joe says the head chef at Arthur's, Tom Windofer, is his favorite cook. "Of course, my wife Mary is also a great cook!" Joe adds.

Richard, from Camden, New Jersey, likes Italian food, too, and his favorite local restaurant is Giuseppe's in Madison, Tennessee. He doesnt cook much either, and his mother's cooking is still his favorite. On tour, he eats a lot of seafood.

William Lee, from Brewton, Alabama, is also partial to Italian food, but on the road, he "eats a lot of gourmet food *and some junk food*." At home, he enjoys food prepared by his wife Luetta. "I'm the world's worst cook," he admits, "but I love to eat!" When he dines out in Nashville, he frequents Ciraco's Italian restaurant, Kobe Steaks Japanese restaurant, Cajun's Wharf and Major Wallaby's.

Duane, who hails from Taylortown, Texas, loves any kind of Southern food. His all-time favorite is fried chicken. He'll cook for himself sometimes, but he'd rather eat a meal prepared by his wife, Norah Lee. On tour, he likes to treat himself to steaks, but in Nashville he often eats at El Chico's Mexican restaurant.

True to form, each of the Oaks submitted separate family recipes. But it all adds up to good eating.

Dolly Parton

Dolly Parton likes to cook, but she admits that she likes eating even better. What does she like eating best? "Potatoes," she once told *Playboy* Magazine. "I'm a starch freak. I'm a junk-food person, too. I like pizza, potato chips, Fritos. My main weakness is overeating." "Now that I'm older and not as active, I have a tendency to gain weight," she explained to *Country Music* magazine. "I always have a good time gaining it and an awful time losing it."

There was a time when Dolly didn't have to worry about gaining weight — instead she was trying to keep it on! That was when she first moved to Nashville in 1964 after having just graduated from Sevier County High School in east Tennessee. After six months of living with her uncle, she got her own apartment and brought home the bacon herself — or whatever she could afford to bring home. "I couldn't afford a car or a telephone, and about the only time I ever ate was when I went out on a date, and I didn't go out on that many dates," she told the Nashville *Tennessean*. "Lots of times my refrigerator was just about empty, except for mustard or turnip greens — things you always keep."

Gradually, Dolly made a name for herself, and a living, in Nashville as a talented songwriter, singer, and promising recording artist. In 1967, Porter Wagoner asked Dolly to join his syndicated television show as a replacement for his departed partner, Norma Jean. They won the Country Music Association's Vocal Duo of the Year award three times — 1968, 1970, and 1971. She and Porter remained a team for seven years.

Not long after ending her partnership with Porter Wagoner, Dolly went on to reach an even wider audience than before with such popular #1 hits as "Here You Come Again," "Islands in the Stream" (her duet with Kenny Rogers), and "9 to 5" — the biggest-selling country music single ever. Of course, Dolly is now recognized not only for her talents as a singer, songwriter, and picker, but also for her television appearances and starring roles in such movies as *9 to 5, Best Little Whorehouse in Texas* and *Rhinestone*. And now she has opened "Dollywood," a theme park with rides, artisans, music and good restaurants, in Pigeon Forge, Tennessee. Dolly is pictured here with one of her chefs from Dollywood.

When she's not busy with her hectic career, Dolly relaxes at home with her husband, Carl Dean. Home is a 23-room plantation-style farmhouse situated on 65 wooded acres, 20 miles outside of Nashville. There, away from the frenetic demands of her career, Dolly can be herself. She does all her own cooking at home in a kitchen that features an old-fashioned, black wood stove with warming ovens. She likes to cook country food and spaghetti (her specialty) especially.

"Home is for us," she once told *Parade* Magazine. "The wig comes off, and I'll just put on a t-shirt and shorts. I'll get out and sit at the edge of the field and read while Carl works. We'll get in the car late at night and go to Taco Bell or Popeye's Famous Fried Chicken, and have a picnic on the front porch, and talk and talk."

Playboy magazine once asked Dolly an interesting question: If she could invite any five people from history to dinner, who would they be? Her reply: "Will Rogers would be my main guest. Beethoven. Bob Hope. Strother Martin. Festus, from 'Gunsmoke.'" What would she serve them? "Fried potatoes and green beans, country-style creamed corn, cornbread and biscuits, pinto beans and turnip greens, meat loaf. I'd probably make up a vanilla pudding. I'd have to fix Beethoven a chef's salad. I don't think he'd want all that grease." If Dolly was dishing it up, he'd probably holler for more.

Minnie Pearl

"Minnie Pearl is uncomplicated. She's apple pie and clothes dried in the sun and the smell of fresh bread baking." So says Mrs. Henry Cannon, and she should know. She created the comic character of Minnie Pearl in 1939. Her portrayal of the gossiping gal from Grinder's Switch has been such a big hit with fans since she joined the Grand Ole Opry in 1940 that Minnie Pearl has become more real to most people than her creator, the former Sarah Ophelia Colley.

She associates Minnie Pearl with down home food like apple pie and fresh-baked bread possibly because she enjoys cooking herself. Cooking, she says, "makes me happy." That wasn't always the case. She remembers one meal in particular as being a fiasco: "the first meal I tried to cook for Henry after we were married." She's better at cooking now, though.

Minnie Pearl had a good teacher in the kitchen when she was growing up. "My most memorable meals are those Mama cooked in Centerville (Tennessee) for our family," she says. "Those were happy times, much gaiety and talking and laughing." Especially happy were the meals around the holidays. Minnie says she thinks Thanksgiving is her favorite holiday meal now, but back then she looked forward to Christmas.

"Christmas breakfast," she once told *Grit* magazine, "included the usual country ham and hot biscuits and featured treats such as scalloped oysters and waffles. Mama baked cakes for weeks. There was fresh coconut, Lady Baltimore, fruitcake, chocolate layer cake and a jam cake made with a gingerbread batter that contained nuts and a filling of homemade blackberry jam, all covered in caramel icing. It was luscious. Our stockings hanging from the mantel were jammed full of nuts, sweets and fresh fruits. I'll always associate Christmas morning with the smell of oranges because that's the only time during winter we ever saw them in Centerville. What with the treats and the feasts, my sister Dixie and I would finish the holiday by eating ourselves sick in the afternoon and picking at leftovers again in the evening."

Today, the food Minnie eats most often is geared toward nutrition and dieting. "I'm trying to stay in those size 12 costumes I've got a closet full of," she wails. Her favorite local restaurant is Tavern on the Row in Nashville. But her favorite place of all to eat is on Curtiswood Lane in Nashville. That's her home address, and it's quite a compliment to her favorite cook, Mary Cannon, who has been her housekeeper and friend for 39 years. Minnie (she doesn't mind if we call her that, everybody does) says her favorite food is eggs. For lunch, she likes to have bacon and eggs. That's not diet food, Minnie knows, but she doesn't care. In fact, she says she chose the recipes included here because "they're all fattening!!"

Main Dishes

THE WHITES' TEXAS CHILI

Patty White, Buck's wife, and mother of Sharon and Cheryl, gave us this recipe. Patty says that when you make Texas chili, you don't add beans. However, Patty serves pinto beans and tortilla chips along with the chili.

¼	pound beef suet
6	pounds lean beef, coarsely cubed (don't use ground beef, it's too fine)
½	cup chili powder
2	tablespoons crushed or ground cumin
2	tablespoons ground oregano
1-2	tablespoons cayenne pepper (this makes it hot!)
4	cloves garlic, minced
2	quarts beef stock or canned beef broth
½	cup masa harina or corn meal
½	cup cold water

Fry suet in chili pot until crisp. Add beef about a pound at a time. Remove each pound as you brown it. Return all meat to chili pot, add seasonings and beef stock or broth. Cover and simmer 1½ to 2 hours. Skim off fat.

Combine masa harina or corn meal with cold water and stir thoroughly into chili. Simmer 30 minutes.

Makes about 3½ quarts.

PEE WEE KING'S FAVORITE CHILI

Pee Wee's favorite has a "try-it-you'll-like-it" ingredient not found in many chili recipes — elbow macaroni.

2	pounds ground beef
	Salt and pepper to taste
1	medium onion, chopped
1	green pepper, chopped
3	ribs celery, chopped
3	tablespoons butter
1	16-ounce can tomatoes
1	16-ounce can tomato sauce
1	cup water
1	teaspoon sugar
½	teaspoon chili powder
2	16-ounce cans kidney beans
1	cup elbow macaroni

In a skillet, brown meat; add salt and pepper to taste. In a separate skillet, saute onions, green pepper and celery in butter. Combine with meat and set aside.

Heat all other ingredients except beans and macaroni in a large pot. Add browned meat and sauteed vegetables. Simmer for 1 hour. Add kidney beans to meat mixture and continue cooking until heated, about 20 minutes.

Meanwhile, cook one cup of elbow macaroni according to package directions. Add macaroni to chili about 10 minutes before serving. Heat and serve.

Makes 6 to 8 servings.

TANYA TUCKER'S CHICKEN CHILI

"Cleans your teeth, curls your hair, and makes you feel like a millionaire," says Tanya!

1-2	onions, chopped
1	clove garlic, minced
3	tablespoons vegetable shortening
1	10-ounce can Ro-Tel tomatoes (canned tomatoes and chilies)
1½	cups stewed tomatoes
3-4	cups kidney beans (better with homemade beans)
1	teaspoon salt
1	bay leaf
1	teaspoon sugar (or 1 packet Sweet-n-low)
¼	cup dry red wine
3	tablespoons chili powder (add more if you like)
4	chicken breast halves
	Salt and pepper to taste
1	tablespoon sherry
2	tablespoons Worcestershire sauce
2	cups chicken broth (if chili is too hot)

In a large pot, saute onions and garlic in shortening until tender. Add Ro-Tel and stewed tomatoes, kidney beans, salt, bay leaf, sugar, wine and chili powder. Simmer together for 1 hour.

Boil chicken breasts for 1 hour in water seasoned with salt and pepper to taste. Drain and reserve broth. Remove skin from cooked chicken and shred by hand or in a food processor. Add to tomato and bean mixture. Simmer for 1 hour. Add sherry and Worcestershire sauce. Add chicken broth if desired for consistency and taste.

Serves "a bunch."

TOM T. HALL'S SKINNY CHILI

We're not sure why Tom calls this chili "skinny," but we sure call it good!

1	pound ground chuck
3	16-ounce cans tomatoes
3	16-ounce cans tomato puree
3	16-ounce cans red kidney beans
1	tablespoon chili powder
1	tablespoons salt
3	16-ounce cans water
1	large onion, finely chopped
1	rib celery, finely chopped
1	bell pepper, finely chopped
4	4-ounce jars chopped pimientos, drained

Brown chuck slowly over low heat until all fat has been rendered. Drain off fat. Add tomatoes, puree, chili powder, salt and water. Simmer slowly over low heat about 3 hours until thick and rich.

Thirty minutes before it is finished, add onion, celery and pimientos to the pot.

Makes 6 servings.

THE STATLER BROTHERS' CHILI

The chili powder you buy at the grocery store is made from chilies that have been dried, roasted, and ground up. It is then usually mixed with cumin or oregano.

1   cup minced onions
1   pound ground beef
2   6-ounce cans tomato paste
½   small box, approximately 1½ ounces, chili powder
3   tablespoons red pepper
     water

In 10-inch skillet, brown onions and ground beef together. Add remaining ingredients one at a time; stir after adding each. Simmer, adding enough water to maintain a desired consistency, for at least three hours over low heat. Stir occasionally.

Makes 4 servings.

RAY STEVENS' MEXICAN CASSEROLE

A spicy Mexican casserole, that's for sure!

1   pound ground beef
1   onion, chopped
1   teaspoon salt
½   teaspoon black pepper
1   bell pepper, diced
1   1¼-ounce package taco seasoning mix
1   16-ounce can tomatoes with juice
1   8-ounce can tomato sauce
1   16-ounce can chili beans, drained
½   teaspoon dried marjoram
1   bay leaf
½   pound sharp cheddar cheese, shredded
     Tostitos corn chips

In a 10-inch skillet, saute beef and onion. Add salt, pepper, bell pepper, seasoning mix, tomatoes, tomato sauce, beans, marjoram and bay leaf. Let simmer for 30 minutes. Remove bay leaf and pour into a 2-quart casserole.

Preheat oven to 350 degrees.

Sprinkle cheese on top. Top with Tostitos. Bake for 20 minutes.

Makes 4 to 6 servings.

EARL THOMAS CONLEY'S CHILI

Earl shares his recipe for lovers of hot and spicy chili.

1	pound ground beef
1	medium onion, chopped
¼-½	bell pepper, chopped
	Worcestershire sauce (dash it over meat)
1	16-ounce can tomato sauce
1	8-ounce can tomatoes
1	tablespoon sugar
	Chili powder
	Sprinkle of garlic salt
	A few crushed red peppers
3	16-ounce cans hot chili beans

Brown beef, onion and bell pepper with Worcestershire sauce. Drain fat and add a little more Worcestershire sauce to taste if desired. Add tomato sauce and tomatoes and stir well. Add sugar and spices and cook for a few minutes, then add chili beans. (If it seems a little thick, or if you want more juice, add water.) Cook over low heat for at least 2 hours.

Makes 8 servings.

GEORGE STRAIT'S CARNE GUISADA

A wonderful Spanish recipe and we suggest you serve it with George's Spanish rice, page 60.

2	tablespoons butter
1	pound round steak, cut in cubes
¼	medium onion, sliced
¼	bell pepper, sliced
1	tablespoon flour
2	cloves garlic, peeled
	Pinch ground cumin
	Pinch coarse-grind black pepper
½	10-ounce can tomatoes

Melt butter in skillet and cook meat, turning occasionally, until brown. Add onion and bell peppers. Add flour and let flour brown while stirring.

Mash garlic, cumin, black pepper and tomatoes. Pour over meat and let simmer for 20 minutes, adding water if necessary for desired thickness.

Makes 2 to 4 servings.

THE WHITES' TEXAS-STYLE ENCHILADAS

In the Whites' house, Buck and his family like a salad of an apple with shredded lettuce and about a tablespoon salad dressing with this meal. A plain lettuce and tomato salad is also good with a little picante sauce added.

Corn Tortillas
2   cups masa harina
1   cup water

In mixing bowl, combine masa harina with water. Mix with hands until paste is moist, but still holds its shape (add more water if needed.) Let stand 15 minutes.

Divide into 12 equal size balls. Dampen slightly. Using a tortilla press or flat baking dish, press each ball of dough between two sheets of wax paper to 6-inch round. Carefully peel off top sheet and place tortilla, paper-side-up, on hot ungreased griddle or skillet. Gently peel off top wax paper. Cook 30 seconds, or until edges begin to dry. Turn, cooking until surface appears puffy. Repeat with remaining dough.

Makes 12 tortillas.

Editors Note: You can buy corn tortillas in the dairy case. Buck believes that "Old El Paso" is the best brand. Also, he claims that it's easier to find them than to find the masa harina in Tennessee and other parts of the U.S.

Enchilada Filling
1   pound sharp cheddar cheese, shredded
     (Kraft is best)
2   medium onions, finely chopped
     Texas Style Chili (or your favorite recipe)

Preheat oven to 350 degrees.

Place equal amount of onion and cheese on each tortilla. Roll the tortilla up. Using Texas-style chili, put ½ inch in bottom of 9 by 13-inch Pyrex baking dish. Place tortillas on top of the chili, and cover the enchiladas with additional Texas-style chili. Cover with additional cheese, and bake until chili is bubbly, and then cook another 15 minutes.

Makes 6 to 12 servings.

THE OAK RIDGE BOYS' MEXICAN PIZZA

Mary Bonsall, wife of tenor and stage spokesman Joe Bonsall, thinks this pizza is "great for summer."

½	cup yellow cornmeal
1½	cups Bisquick baking mix
½	cup cold water
1	pound ground beef
1	4-ounce can whole green chilies, drained, seeded and chopped
1	1¼-ounce envelope taco seasoning mix
¾	cup water
½	16-ounce can refried beans
1½	cups shredded cheddar cheese
1	cup shredded lettuce
2	medium tomatoes, chopped
½	cup chopped onion
	Taco sauce (optional)

Preheat oven to 425 degrees.

Mix cornmeal, Bisquick and ½ cup water until soft dough forms. Roll or pat into 12-inch circle on ungreased cookie sheet, forming ½-inch-high rim. Bake for 10 to 15 minutes or until golden brown. Remove from oven.

Reduce oven temperature to 350 degrees.

In a skillet, cook ground beef over medium heat, stirring, until brown; drain fat. Stir in chilies, seasoning mix and ¾ cup water. Heat to boiling, stirring frequently; reduce heat. Simmer uncovered for 5 to 10 minutes.

Spread beans over baked crust, top with beef mixture; sprinkle with cheese. Bake 10 minutes longer. Top with lettuce, tomatoes and onion. Serve with taco sauce, if desired.

Makes 6 servings.

BOBBY BARE'S PASTA WITH GARLIC AND OIL

Bobby is a pasta fan. These two recipes are among his favorites. This one is simple, quick and scrumptious.

1	pound linguini
¾	cup olive oil
1½	cloves garlic, minced
¼	cup butter, cut up
	Salt
	Peppercorns, ground

Cook linguini according to package directions.

While pasta is cooking, put olive oil in a frying pan and to this add the garlic and brown. After linguini is cooked, remove from heat and drain. Add to the oil and garlic, stir in butter and salt and pepper to taste. Toss. Serve immediately.

Makes 4 servings.

B. J. THOMAS' FETTUCINE ALFREDO

One secret to successful fettucine is to toss eggs, cream, butter and cheese quickly with the fettucine noodles – about 2 minutes – and serve immediately.

12	ounces fettucine noodles
	Pinch salt
2	egg yolks
⅔	cup half-and-half
½	cup butter, cut up in chunks
½	cup grated Parmesan cheese

Bring to a boil 5 quarts of water. Add fettucine noodles and a pinch of salt, if desired. Boil until noodles are just done, about 7 minutes. While noodles are cooking, beat egg yolks and add to half-and-half. Drain fettucine and place back in pan. Return pan to medium heat. Pour egg yolk and half-and-half mixture over fettucine and mix quickly. Immediately add butter and Parmesan cheese. Stir well until butter is melted. Serve immediately.

Makes 5 servings.

Editors Note: When cooking fettucine for guests, you may want to boil the noodles, drain and mix lightly with about ⅓ of the butter and set aside. When ready to serve, complete the recipe.

LEE GREENWOOD'S SPAGHETTI SAUCE

Lee tells us that he sometimes substitutes two pounds of ground beef shaped into meatballs for the meat in this recipe. "Simply mix the beef with 1 beaten egg, 1 cup bread crumbs and salt, pepper, garlic salt and chopped parsley to taste. Shape into 2-inch balls and brown in skillet. Gently add to the spaghetti sauce, cook 3 hours and serve."

1	16-ounce can whole tomatoes, coarsely chopped (include juice)
1	8-ounce can tomato sauce
1	6-ounce can tomato paste
2	cups water
1	medium onion, chopped
3	tablespoons chopped fresh parsley
	Salt and pepper to taste
3	garlic cloves, chopped
	Dried oregano to taste (optional)
¼	cup chopped onion
2	pounds meat from a combination of pork chops, ribs and chicken, diced
3	tablespoons olive oil or vegetable oil

Combine all ingredients except onion, meat and oil in large saucepan or pot and heat. Meanwhile, brown chopped onion and the combination of meat in oil. Then add everything including oil to the sauce and simmer for 3 hours, stirring occasionally. Add water if necessary, for desired thickness.

Serve over cooked spaghetti.

Makes 6 to 8 cups of meat sauce.

THE OAK RIDGE BOYS' LASAGNA

Bass singer Richard Sterban's mother, Victoria, makes this lasagna, a favorite of Richard's.

1	small onion, chopped
4	tablespoons olive oil or vegetable oil
1	clove garlic, minced
1½	pounds ground beef
1	29-ounce can tomato puree
2	6-ounce cans tomato paste
2	6-ounce cans water
2	teaspoons salt
½	teaspoon black pepper
½	teaspoon dried oregano
¼	teaspoon sugar
1	pound lasagna noodles
6	quarts boiling water
1	pound ricotta cheese or cottage cheese
8	ounces mozzarella cheese, sliced thinly
½	cup grated Parmesan cheese
4	eggs, hard-cooked, sliced (optional)

In a large pan on medium heat, cook onions and garlic in 3 tablespoons oil until golden brown; add beef, cook until brown and crumbly. Stir in tomato puree; add tomato paste, water, 1 teaspoon salt, pepper, oregano and sugar. Cover and simmer for about 1½ hours.

When sauce is finished, cook lasagna in 6 quarts boiling water with 1 teaspoon salt and 1 tablespoon oil. Boil 15 minutes, drain, and run under cold water.

Preheat oven to 350 degrees.

In a 9 by 13-inch baking dish, spread a thin layer of the tomato sauce and then put a layer of lasagna noodles, a layer of ricotta cheese, mozzarella cheese and finally a layer of hard-boiled eggs if desired. Repeat for 3 layers. End with noodles topped with tomato sauce and sprinkled with Parmesan cheese. Cover with foil and bake for about 45 minutes.

Makes 6 servings.

BOBBY BARE'S PASTA WITH CARBONARA SAUCE

Bobby's recipe is an excellent variation of fettucine recipes.

1	pound fettucine or spaghetti
6	quarts water
3	tablespoons salt
4	eggs
¼	cup heavy cream
¼	cup butter or margarine
2	3½-ounce packages sliced Hormel pepperoni
1	cup grated Parmesan cheese
½	cup chopped fresh parsley
	Pepper to taste

Cook pasta according to package directions in salted water. Drain well.

Preheat oven to 300 degrees.

Eggs, butter or margarine and cream must be at room temperature. Beat together eggs and cream until blended. Turn pasta into a heated oven-proof serving dish and toss with butter and pepperoni. Pour egg mixture over and toss. Add cheese, parsley, pepper and toss gently to mix. Bake for 15 minutes, or until bubbling.

Makes 4 to 5 servings.

BRENDA LEE'S DILLED STEAK ROLL-UPS

Brenda was introduced to this interesting combination of foods while on a visit to Japan. The ginger in the marinade is her idea.

1½	pounds flank steak
⅓	cup soy sauce
1	tablespoon sugar
⅓	cup dill pickle liquid
¼	teaspoon ground ginger
6	medium carrots, cut in 1½-inch slices
6	dill pickles, cut in strips
4	tablespoons melted butter
	Party rye bread

Wrap flank steak in plastic wrap and place in freezer until it just starts to harden, approximately 15 minutes. Remove steak from freezer, trim fat and discard. Slice steak on a diagonal into ¼-inch-thick slices. In a shallow bowl large enough to hold steak slices, combine soy sauce, sugar, dill pickle liquid and ginger. Add steak to marinade, toss, cover and chill for 2 hours. Turn occasionally. Meanwhile, cook carrots unti tender-crisp.

Remove marinated steak slices from refrigerator. On each steak slice place one carrot and one pickle slice. Roll up and fasten with a metal skewer. Brush with melted butter. Grill or broil 4 inches from heat for approximately 5 minutes, turning once, or until desired doneness is attained. Serve with party rye slices.

Makes 4 servings.

BARBARA MANDRELL'S CHINESE PEPPER STEAK

A favorite of Barbara's. But then she tells us that "my favorite meal is whatever I'm eating — just as my favorite record is always my latest release."

2-2½ pounds sirloin steak
1   tablespoon vegetable shortening or oil
4   large bell peppers, sliced
3   medium yellow onions, sliced
2   tablespoons soy sauce
2½   tablespoons Worcestershire sauce
        Dash chili powder
2   ¾-ounce packages instant brown gravy
1   8-ounce can water chestnuts, halved
2   ribs celery, cut in bite-size pieces
1   14-ounce can bean sprouts (optional)
        Salt and pepper
        Quick-cooking rice

Cut steak into bite-size strips. Set aside.

In a large pan (preferably iron) heat oil and fry the peppers and onions, just until crisp. At the same time, braise steak in a second frying pan with soy sauce and Worcestershire sauce. Add a dash of chili powder to the meat. Add the steak and its juices to the peppers and onions. Simmer.

Prepare the instant brown gravy according to package directions; add to the meat and vegetables. Add water chestnuts, celery and bean sprouts. Heat through. Salt and pepper to taste.

To complete dish, prepare enough quick-cooking rice according to package directions to make about 8 cups. Mound rice on individual serving plates and spoon meat mixture over it.

Makes 9 to 12 servings.

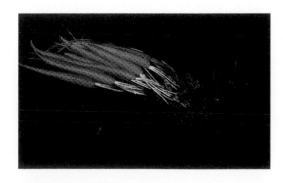

CONWAY TWITTY'S TERIYAKI STEAK WITH BACON-FRIED RICE

If Conway asks Mickey, his wife, to fix his favorite dish, this is it! Mickey says, "This teriyaki steak is a pretty casual recipe because I just do it, I don't think about it. I'm not sure how I came up with this recipe, it just developed."

2	tablespoons butter
6	¼-inch thick slices of beef tenderloin
	Salt and pepper
½	cup bottled teriyaki sauce (more if desired)

Heat butter in a large Teflon skillet until hot. Place steak slices in the butter and brown on both sides. Sprinkle with salt and pepper to taste. Keep skillet very hot as steak cooks. Pour teriyaki sauce over steak and remove pan from burner. Let sauce seep into the steak. Transfer steak and sauce to a hot platter.

Makes 6 servings.

Bacon-fried rice:

2	cups raw rice
1	pound bacon
	Bacon drippings
3	eggs, lightly beaten
1	bunch green onions, including tops, chopped
1	8-ounce can water chestnuts, drained and chopped
½	cup hot water
½	cup soy sauce, or to taste

Prepare rice according to package directions. Cook the bacon, either in skillet or a microwave until crisp. Crumble and set aside. Reserve bacon drippings.

Heat 2 tablespoons of bacon drippings in a large skillet or electric frying pan. Add the eggs and scramble; add bacon, rice, onions and water chestnuts. Mix soy sauce and hot water together and pour over rice mixture. Heat, stirring, until thoroughly hot and mixed. Serve with steak.

Makes 6 servings.

T. G. SHEPPARD'S CABBAGE ROLLS

"If you prefer, place a dollop of sour cream atop each cabbage roll as they are served," says T.G.

½   *pound pork sausage*
2   *pounds ground beef*
1   *medium onion, chopped*
     Salt and pepper to taste
¼   *teaspoon dried thyme*
1   *7-ounce box Minute Rice, uncooked*
2   *medium heads cabbage (about 4 pounds)*
1   *16-ounce can sauerkraut, drained*
1   *10-ounce can tomato juice*

Brown sausage and beef in large skillet over medium heat. Add onion and cook for 5 minutes. Season with salt, pepper and thyme. Cover mixture with Minute Rice and mix with the meat mixture. Turn off the heat and cover.

Preheat oven to 350 degrees.

Section the cabbage, keeping leaves whole. Drain fat from meat mixture. Divide the meat mixture evenly among 12 to 16 leaves, fold ends inside, roll up and place each with open end down in a large baking dish. Cover the filled leaves with sauerkraut and pour tomato juice over all. Bake for 2 hours.

Makes 8 servings.

MEL TILLIS' CORNED BEEF AND CABBAGE

Mel likes to serve his corned beef and cabbage with potato salad, corn bread, sliced tomatoes and onions for a fine full meal.

2   pounds brisket of beef
     Salt and pepper
     Vegetable oil
2   cups water
1   head cabbage

Salt and pepper brisket. Brown in oil in skillet over high heat. Place water in a pressure cooker. Now place the brisket in the cooker and let pressure rise to 15 lb./sq. in. or 1.05 kg./sq. cm. When pressure is built, time for 45 minutes.

Quarter the cabbage and place on top of brisket after cooking brisket 45 minutes. Add additional water if necessary. Let build up again to same pressure and cook an additional 8 minutes.

Always read instructions carefully when using a pressure cooker and follow them closely.

Makes 4 to 6 servings.

Editors Note: We suggest you put the liquid for the pressure cooker in first so you do not forget it. A pressure cooker works by producing steam from the liquid and without it there will be a disaster. If you do not have a pressure cooker, simmer brisket in 3 cups of water in a tightly covered pot for approximatley 2 hours. Then place cabbage on brisket, cover and simmer an additional 20 to 30 minutes.

THE OAK RIDGE BOYS' DRY BEEF PIE

This variation of an old-fashioned dish comes from Joe Bonsall's mother.

       Unbaked pastry for 2-crust pie
2-3   pounds potatoes
2   large onions
       Salt to taste
¼   pound dry or chipped beef
½   cup margarine, softened
¼   cup milk
       Dash pepper

Prepare pie crust for a 2-crust pie.

Slice potatoes and onions and boil in salted water until tender but still firm.

Preheat oven to 350 degrees.

Mix dry beef, margarine, milk and pepper with the potatoes and onions. Mix well. Spoon mixture into pie crust, and top with the second pie crust. Crimp edges and seal. Bake for 1 hour, or until golden brown.

Makes 6 servings.

THE OAK RIDGE BOYS' GROUND BEEF AND BEAN CASSEROLE

A specialty of the Duane Allen home — this casserole is one of their many favorites.

½ pound ground beef
½ cup chopped onion
¼ cup diced green pepper
2 teaspoons chili powder
1 16-ounce can pork and beans
3 cups cooked macaroni
2 cups shredded sharp cheddar cheese
½ cup milk
½ teaspoon salt
Green pepper rings, (optional)

Preheat oven to 400 degrees.

Brown beef, onion and green pepper with chili powder until tender; add beans, macaroni, cheese, milk and salt.

Pour into 1½-quart casserole. Bake for 30 minutes. Stir; garnish with green pepper rings, if desired.

Makes 4 to 6 servings.

LITTLE JIMMY DICKENS' BEEF AND EGG NOODLES

The egg noodles may be prepared ahead of time, if desired and frozen in a covered container. Thaw when ready to use. These would be good used in any recipe calling for egg noodles.

3 eggs, beaten
6 tablespoons milk
2 teaspoons salt
3 cups all-purpose flour
1 pound boiling beef (stew meat is good)
6 cups water

Combine eggs, milk and 1 teaspoon salt. Add flour to make stiff dough. Roll very thin on floured surface. Let stand 20 minutes. Roll up loosely and cut in ¼-inch slices. Unroll each slice, spread out flat and let dry 2 hours.

Meanwhile, place meat in boiling water and add remaining teaspoon salt. Return to boiling, reduce heat slightly and continue meat boiling for 2 hours. Add additional water if water cooks down too much.

When beef is cooked, drop noodles into boiling water with meat and cook over low heat for 10 minutes.

Makes 5 to 6 servings.

DOLLY PARTON'S COWBOY BEANS

When you visit "Dollywood" in Tennessee, you'll find this favorite dish at the Chuckwagon.

1	pound ground beef
2	medium onions, finely chopped
1	small bell pepper, finely chopped
2	16-ounce cans pork and beans, or 4 cups fresh cooked October beans
2	cups ketchup
1	teaspoon vinegar
¼	cup brown sugar
2	teaspoons prepared mustard
1	teaspoon salt
1	teaspoon pepper

Brown ground beef, onions and pepper in a 10-inch skillet. Add remaining ingredients. Pour into baking dish and bake at 350 degrees for about 15 to 20 minutes or until mixture is bubbly.

Serves 8 to 10.

CHERYL WHITE'S SLUMGULION CASSEROLE

For slumgulion lovers everywhere!

2	medium onions, chopped
1	tablespoon Crisco shortening
1	pound ground beef
2	tablespoons chili powder
1	15-ounce can tomato sauce
4	cups water
4	cups noodles
1	10¾-ounce can cream of mushroom soup
1	16-ounce can whole kernel corn
1	cup shredded cheddar cheese

Saute onions in shortening in skillet. Add ground beef and brown.

Preheat oven to 350 degrees.

Add remaining ingredients, except cheese, and cook over medium heat until noodles are tender. Place mixture in greased 3-quart baking dish or casserole and cover with cheese. Bake until cheese melts, about 20-25 minutes.

Makes 4 to 6 servings.

THE STATLER BROTHERS' IMPOSSIBLE CHEESEBURGER PIE

This is an easy recipe that gives the ordinary cheeseburger glamour.

1	pound ground beef
1½	cups chopped onion
½	teaspoon salt
¼	teaspoon pepper
1	cup shredded cheddar cheese
1½	cup milk
¾	cup Bisquick baking mix
3	eggs

Preheat oven to 400 degrees.

Lightly grease 10-inch pie plate. In skillet over medium heat, brown ground beef and onions; drain. Stir in salt and pepper. Spread in pie plate; sprinkle evenly with cheese.

Beat remaining ingredients until smooth, 15 seconds in blender on high speed or one minute with hand beater. Pour over cheese. Bake until golden brown and knife inserted in center comes out clean, about 30 minutes. Let stand 5 minutes before cutting. Refrigerate leftover pie for future use.

Makes 6 to 8 servings.

TANYA TUCKER'S STROGANOFF IN A FLASH

Tanya enjoys sharing cooking with friends and this recipe is also a favorite of her friend Mary Farr.

2	pounds ground beef
1	large onion, chopped
1	teaspoon garlic powder
1	teaspoon black pepper
1	2½-ounce jar sliced mushrooms
1	10¾-ounce can cream of mushroom soup, undiluted
1	10¾-ounce can cream of celery soup, undiluted
1	1-ounce package egg noodles

In large skillet, brown beef. Add onion, garlic powder, pepper, mushrooms and soups. Heat thoroughly.

Prepare egg noodles according to package directions. Drain. Serve meat sauce over noodles.

Makes 6 to 8 servings.

CONWAY TWITTY'S TWITTY-BURGERS

Conway was in Hawaii when it occurred to him that a pineapple ring would really top off a hamburger – and make it a Twitty Burger!

Batter
¾   cup sifted all-purpose flour
1   tablespoon sugar
1   tablespoon melted butter
¼   cup lukewarm water
⅛   teaspoon salt
1   egg, beaten
4   pineapple slices
    Oil for deep frying

Sift flour and sugar into bowl. Stir in melted butter and water. Mix well. Add salt and egg; combine well. Dip pineapple slices into batter and deep fry them.

Burgers
4   large ground sirloin patties
    salt and pepper to taste
4   large sesame seed buns
    mayonnaise
8   slices bacon, fried crisp
8   very thin slices tomato

Grill patties to individual taste, add salt and pepper. Toast sesame seed buns if desired; spread both sides of bun with mayonnaise. Build the sandwich by placing the cooked patty on the bun and topping it with 2 slices of bacon and 2 tomato slices. Finish it off with the fried pineapple slice and the top of the bun.

Makes 4 servings.

JERRY REED'S MEAT LOAF

Ask Jerry what will round out his favorite meal of dried beans, fried okra, fried corn, mashed potatoes, sliced onions and iced tea and he'll tell you: this meatloaf recipe!

1   pound ground round
2   cups Corn Flakes cereal, crushed
1   cup raw rice
½   cup diced bell pepper
1   onion, diced
1   tomato, diced
1   6-ounce can tomato sauce

Preheat oven to 375 degrees.

Mix all ingredients thoroughly. Form into a loaf and place in a lightly greased casserole dish. Bake until loaf begins to brown on the edges, approximately 45 minutes.

Makes 4 servings.

LEE GREENWOOD'S CHEDDAR MEATLOAF

*A true American standby, this
meatloaf is for cheese lovers.*

1½   pounds lean ground beef
½   cup ketchup
1   egg
1   cup bread crumbs
1   1¼-ounce package Lipton onion soup mix
2   cups shredded cheddar cheese

Preheat oven to 350 degrees.

In a bowl, mix all ingredients except cheese. Take one-half of the
mixture and shape into a loaf. Place cheese on top of loaf. Add the
remaining meat to cover cheese, pressing all sides so that the cheese
is totally covered inside the loaf. Place in lightly greased loaf pan or
baking dish. Bake for 1 hour and 15 minutes.

Makes 4 to 6 servings.

ALABAMA'S BARBEQUE MAGNIFIQUE

*You can baste meat with many
mixtures, but Mark Herndon's
combination of beer, dijon
mustard and peanut butter is
quite a new sauce in anyone's
recipe file!*

1   12-ounce can Budweiser beer
3   tablespoons Dijon-style mustard
2   tablespoons peanut butter
      Dash cayenne pepper
      Dash lemon pepper seasoning
      Dash Worcestershire sauce
      Dash garlic salt

Heat all ingredients in a saucepan. Bring to a boil and then simmer until
consistency is right to brush on hamburgers and steaks. Use sauce for
basting meat while it cooks. Enough sauce for 4 to 6 servings.

THE STATLER BROTHERS' BAR-B-QUE FLATJACKS

*We suggest a salad and green
vegetable with this spicy and tasty
casserole.*

1   pound ground beef
¼   cup chopped onion
½   cup barbeque sauce
½   teaspoon Tabasco
1   10-ounce can refrigerated biscuits
1   cup shredded cheddar cheese

Preheat oven to 375 degrees.

In large frying pan, brown ground beef and onion; drain and stir in
barbeque sauce and Tabasco. Simmer.

Butter a 13 by 9-inch baking pan.

Press the biscuits over the bottom and sides of the pan to form a crust.
Spread hot meat mixture over crust and sprinkle with cheese. Bake
for 20 minutes.

Makes 6 servings.

THE STATLER BROTHERS' BARBECUED BEEF

Barbecue comes in a multitude of varieties and this one is another favorite dish.

¾ cup water
2 pounds round steak, cut in 1-inch chunks
½ cup ketchup
½ cup chili sauce
4 teaspoons brown sugar
1 tablespoon cider vinegar
½ teaspoon salt
1 medium onion, minced

About 1½ hours before serving, mix water and all other ingredients in large skillet. Cover and let stand 30 minutes in refrigerator.

Cook mixture, covered, over medium low heat about 50 minutes or until steak is fork-tender.

Makes 6 servings.

HELEN CORNELIUS' SPICY RIB-EYE BEEF

Helen garnishes this roast with peach or apricot halves, hot pepper jelly and fresh sprigs of parsley.

1 6-pound boneless beef rib eye roast
⅓-½ cup coarse or cracked pepper
½ teaspoon ground cardamon
1 cup soy sauce
¾ cup red wine vinegar
1 tablespoon tomato paste
1 teaspoon paprika
½ teaspoon garlic powder

Trim excess fat from roast. Combine pepper and cardamon; pat onto roast. Combine next 5 ingredients; pour over roast. Cover. Marinate overnight or at least 8 hours in refrigerator, turning meat occasionally.

Preheat oven to 325 degrees.

Remove roast from marinade and discard marinade. Wrap roast in foil and place in a shallow baking pan. Insert meat thermometer, making an opening so that thermometer does not touch foil. Bake for 2 hours or until thermometer registers 140 degrees (rare) or 160 degrees (medium).

Makes 12 servings.

THE STATLER BROTHERS' BARBEQUE SAUCE

Use this sauce (note how much it yields) to marinate beef, pork or chicken. It is also good brushed on the meats.

2   stalks celery, finely chopped
2   medium onions, finely chopped
½   cup water
1   gallon ketchup
5   ounces Worcestershire sauce
¼   cup vinegar
    Juice of one lemon
1½ ounces chili powder
1   8-ounce jar prepared mustard
1   pound brown sugar

Place celery and onions in saucepan with water. Simmer until tender. Drain.

In large saucepan, combine all ingredients. Mix thoroughly. Simmer, stirring occasionally, until sugar is melted and mixture is hot, approximately 20 minutes. If sauce is not sweet enough, add white sugar to desired taste.

Makes approximately 5 quarts.

EARL THOMAS CONLEY'S BEEF STEW

Earl's favorite meal of the day is lunch, and his favorite dish is a hearty bowl of beef stew.

2   tablespoons butter
2   tablespoons vegetable oil
1   pound beef stew meat, cut up in small pieces
1   medium onion, chopped
½   bell pepper, chopped
     Worcestershire sauce – dash it over meat
¾   15-ounce can tomato sauce
4-5 potatoes, diced
2-3 carrots, diced
1   16-ounce can Veg-all (canned mixed vegetables)
¾   16-ounce can green beans, drained
¾   8-ounce can corn, drained
     Salt and pepper

Heat butter and oil in a skillet and brown meat, onion, bell pepper and Worcestershire sauce to taste. Add tomato sauce, simmer for a few minutes. Meanwhile, cook potatoes and carrots in water until tender; drain and add other vegetables. Add skillet ingredients to vegetables and cook on low heat until hot. Season with salt and pepper. Serve with corn muffins.

Makes 8 servings.

Editors Note: One pound of fresh green beans, cut into one-inch pieces and cooked, may be used in place of canned green beans. Two ears of fresh corn, cooked and with kernels removed from cob, may be substituted for canned corn.

M-M-MEL TILLIS' HAMBURGER STEW

This is a great "left-over" recipe. Cut up odds and ends of vegetables you have and toss them in!

2   pounds ground beef
4-5   large carrots, thinly sliced
3-4   large potatoes, cubed
1   large onion, chopped
        Salt and pepper to taste
        Water
1   10-ounce package frozen sliced okra or 9 — 10 fresh okra pods
6   servings cooked rice (optional)

Brown beef in skillet; drain off grease. Place ground beef in large pot. Add carrots, potatoes, onion, salt and pepper. Cover ingredients with water and cook with lid on for 30 minutes over medium heat. Add okra. Cover and cook an additional 15 minutes. Add additional water while cooking if necessary. Serve over rice, if desired.

Makes 6 servings.

BILL ANDERSON'S BEEF STEW

Bill's beef stew is perfect with a tossed salad and your favorite bread for a football party buffet with friends.

6   tablespoons vegetable shortening
3   pounds sirloin tip roast, cut into bite-size pieces
2   medium yellow onions, chopped
5   cups water
1½   cups red wine
2   beef bouillon cubes
2   tablespoons minced garlic
        Few sprigs parsley
1   bay leaf
        Dash thyme
1½   teaspoons salt
¼   teaspoon pepper
10   medium potatoes, peeled and chopped
10   medium carrots, peeled and sliced
10   small white onions
2   medium green peppers, cut into chunks
2   medium tomatoes, cut into chunks

Heat shortening in heavy 10 to 12-inch skillet. Add meat and cook until brown. Remove meat from skillet with slotted spoon; add onions to skillet and saute until limp. Return meat to skillet. Add water, wine, bouillon cubes, garlic, parsley, bay leaf, thyme, salt and pepper. Bring to boil; reduce heat, cover and cook slowly 1½ hours.

Add potatoes, carrots and onions to skillet. Cook gently 1 hour or until tender. Twenty minutes before end of cooking time, add peppers and tomatoes. Thicken gravy with flour if desired.

Makes 6 to 8 servings.

TANYA TUCKER'S CHICKEN FRIED STEAK

Here is Tanya's hint to accompany this real Southern favorite: "For the taters, I like to mix in ½ cup of sour cream — it gives them a great taste!"

2   pounds minute steaks, or pounded beef filet
1   16-ounce can evaporated milk
    All-purpose flour (for dredging)
    Vegetable oil for frying
¼   cup all-purpose flour
1   10¾-ounce can Campbell's beef consomme
1   tablespoon sweet vermouth

Tenderize meat if needed, and dip in evaporated milk and then into flour that has been seasoned with salt and pepper. Repeat once (reserve milk for later.) Fry in 1 inch hot oil over medium-high heat until golden brown or to desired crispness. Take ¼ cup of drippings, browned or burned, and mix with ¼ cup of flour (if grease has been "cooked" too much, use ¼ cup of butter or margarine to begin gravy instead of drippings) and stir until thoroughly mixed.

Add beef consomme and remainder of evaporated milk. You may wish to use additional milk to establish the thickness of the gravy that you prefer. Bring mixture to a very light boil and add sweet vermouth (you may wish to use more to taste.) *Do not salt the gravy!* The consomme adds all the taste and salt you need, but you may wish to season with pepper. Serve gravy hot with fried steaks and mashed 'taters!

Makes 6 servings.

THE STATLER BROTHERS' IMPOSSIBLE REUBEN PIE

Use any cheese you like for this main-dish pie — we suggest Swiss, Jack or cheddar. And this Reuben Pie isn't impossible to make . . . it's just impossibly good!

1   8-ounce can corned beef, diced
4   ounces (1 cup) of any cheese preferred, shredded
1   8-ounce can sauerkraut, well-drained
1   cup milk
⅓   cup mayonnaise
2   tablespoons chili sauce
¾   cup Bisquick baking mix
3   large eggs, beaten

Preheat oven to 350 degrees.

Butter a glass 9-inch pie plate. Cover bottom of pie plate with corned beef. Sprinkle grated cheese evenly over top of corned beef. Place sauerkraut over cheese. In bowl, combine remaining ingredients and pour over top of corned beef, cheese and kraut.

Bake 30 minutes. Let stand about 5 minutes before serving.

Makes 6 to 8 servings.

CONWAY TWITTY'S BAKED HAM WITH PEACH HONEY GLAZE

Conway tells us that he and wife Mickey invented this recipe after a friend brought over some pear honey one day. They liked it so much that they thought peach honey might be good, too. This is the recipe they make every year during peach season and they always save a jar or two for baking with a party ham.

4   fresh peaches
¾   cup sugar
8   ounces unsweetened crushed pineapple
1   tablespoon lemon juice
1   3-pound precooked ham
     Maraschino cherries (if desired)

Preheat oven to 350 degrees.

Wash, peel and chop peaches. To make peach honey glaze, place peaches in a saucepan with sugar, pineapple and lemon juice. Bring to a boil, lower heat and simmer, uncovered, stirring frequently, for about 30 minutes.

Meanwhile, place the ham, fat side up with rind removed, in an open roasting pan. Score the top side in a diamond pattern and cover with the peach honey glaze and decorate with maraschino cherries, if desired, before cooking. Bake, allowing 10 minutes per pound.

Serves up to 30.

Editors Note: To score the ham, simply cut ¼ inch deep through fat with a sharp knife. Cut diagonally one way and then the other to form a diamond pattern.

MINNIE PEARL'S SPARERIBS AND SAUERKRAUT

This recipe is an invention of Mary Cannon, Minnie's longtime friend and housekeeper. Minnie says that "as if this were not fattening enough, we like to serve cooked noodles with the kraut and ribs on top of the noodles. We recommend this for daytime eating because this dish is so rich!"

3   pounds pork spareribs
2   27-ounce cans sauerkraut
2   cans water (54 ounces)
     Salt and cayenne pepper to taste

Preheat oven to 350 degrees.

Brown spareribs in a heavy skillet with small amount of fat. Place sauerkraut in a Dutch oven. Add water. Add seasonings. Place ribs on top of kraut. Cook covered for 2 hours.

Makes 6 servings.

THE STATLER BROTHERS' BAKED PORK TENDERLOIN AND GRAVY

We suggest you try this pork tenderloin served with sauteed apples.

1   pork tenderloin cut into serving pieces
All-purpose flour
Salt and pepper to taste
Water (as needed)

Preheat oven to 375 degrees.

Coat tenderloin well in flour. Place floured pieces of tenderloin into large, well-greased baking dish. Salt and pepper to taste. Place in oven and bake until tenderloin is brown on one side, then turn and let brown on other side. When well browned, about 10 mintues for each side, cover with water and let bake.

As broth cooks down, add more water until meat is tender. Bake approximately 2 to 3 hours, depending on thickness of meat. Remove meat from baking dish to warm platter.

Make a paste of 2 tablespoons flour and water to make a thin to medium consistency. Gradually add the flour mixture to the meat broth to thicken, stirring constantly, until gravy is of the consistency you prefer. You may thicken the gravy over medium heat on top of the range if your baking dish can be used on a burner. Pour ½ gravy over meat and serve the rest on the side.

Makes 4 servings.

TAMMY WYNETTE'S SOUTHERN STUFFED BELL PEPPERS

This recipe is a very good way to use your leftover baked ham!

1   pan cooked cornbread (8 by 12-inch pan)
1   16-ounce can niblet corn, drained
1   16-ounce can stewed tomatoes, chopped
1   16-ounce can LeSueur peas, drained
1-2   pounds canned ham, cut into 1-inch squares
6   large bell peppers, cored, parboiled
6   strips bacon

Preheat oven to 300 degrees.

Crumble cornbread into large mixing bowl. Add corn, tomatoes and peas. Mix until evenly moist. Add ham and mix thoroughly. Stuff mixture into bell peppers and place in large glass baking dish. Spoon excess stuffing around peppers and place one strip of bacon on top of each pepper. Bake for 40 minutes.

Makes 6 servings.

BRENDA LEE'S CHINESE PORK AND VEGGIES

A favorite "low-calorie" meal of Brenda's. Each delicious serving has less than 400 calories.

½	pound lean pork
1	cup quick meat broth (see Brenda's recipe, page 00)
¼	cup soy sauce
1	teaspoon cider vinegar
½	teaspoon MSG
¼	teaspoon non-caloric sweetener
1	clove garlic, cut in half with wooden pick inserted in each half
4	ribs celery, cut in 1-inch pieces
3	medium onions, about ½ pound, chopped
¼	pound spinach, washed and cut into large shreds
1	green pepper, cut in bite-size pieces
1	cup cooked rice (optional)

Set out a heavy skillet having a tight-fitting cover. Wipe pork with a clean, damp cloth and cut into thin strips. Heat the skillet over medium heat. Add the meat strips and brown, occasionally moving and turning pieces with a fork.

Add ½ cup meat broth to skillet. Add soy sauce, vinegar, MSG, sweetener and garlic halves. Cover and simmer for 20 minutes or until meat is tender.

Meanwhile, prepare celery, onions, spinach and pepper.

When meat is almost tender, add to the skillet the remaining meat broth, celery, onion and spinach. Partially cover skillet and cook until meat is tender, about 5 or 6 minutes. Add green pepper and cook 1 minute longer. (Vegetables should be crisp.) Remove garlic and serve over cooked rice.

Makes 2 servings.

BRENDA LEE'S STUFFED PORK CHOPS

"Invite your record producer to dinner for this recipe!" says Brenda, — "or your boss!"

8	pork chops, 1 to 1¼ inch thick (ask your butcher to cut "little pockets" for stuffing)
1	medium-sized apple, peeled, cored and diced (about 1 cup)
2	tablespoons lemon juice
2	cups soft bread crumbs (make from about 2 slices bread)
1	teaspoon salt
1	teaspoon celery seed
¼	teaspoon MSG
⅛	teaspoon pepper
¼	cup butter or margarine
½	cup chopped onions
¼	cup apple cider (or less)
2	teaspoons fat or shortening

Set out a large shallow baking dish, 9 x 14 inch with aluminum foil to cover. Wipe chops with a clean, damp cloth. Sprinkle apple with lemon juice. In a bowl, mix apple, bread crumbs, salt, celery seed, MSG and pepper. Set aside.

Over low heat, melt butter in a saucepan. Add onions. Cook over medium heat until translucent, occasionally moving with a spoon. Add to apple mixture and toss lightly with apple cider; use just enough cider to barely moisten bread crumbs. Fill pocket of each chop with stuffing.

Preheat oven to 350 degrees.

In a heavy skillet over medium heat, melt fat. Brown chops on both sides. Remove chops to baking dish. Cover with aluminum foil and bake for 1 hour or until pork is tender and thoroughly cooked. (Just to be sure of doneness, cut a slit near the bone — no pink color should be visible.)

Makes 8 servings.

B. J. THOMAS' VEAL SCALLOPINI

Scallopini refers to thin slices of meat, usually veal, that are sauteed or coated with flour and fried. B.J.'s is an interesting variation.

1½	pounds veal round steak
¼	cup all-purpose flour
½	teaspoon salt
	Dash of pepper
1	teaspoon paprika
2	tablespoons vegetable shortening
1	3-ounce can sliced broiled mushrooms
1	teaspoon beef-flavored gravy base
½	cup tomato sauce
2	tablespoons chopped green pepper
4	ounces medium-wide noodles
	Parmesan cheese

Preheat oven to 350 degrees.

Pound veal with mallet until approximately ¼-inch in thickness. Cut into serving pieces. Coat veal in flour seasoned with salt, pepper and paprika. Brown veal in skillet in hot melted shortening. Drain. Place veal in baking dish.

Drain mushrooms, reserving the liquid. Set the mushrooms aside. Add water to the mushroom liquid to make ½ cup; heat until liquid boils. Stir in gravy base and pour over the veal. Bake, covered, for 30 minutes. Combine tomato sauce, green pepper and mushrooms; pour over veal and bake, uncovered, for 15 minutes more.

Cook noodles until tender in large amount of boiling salted water; drain. Baste meat with sauce just before serving and sprinkle with Parmesan cheese. Serve with noodles.

Makes 4 to 6 servings.

THE JUDDS' CORN DOGS

You've feasted on them at the ball park, now, with Wynonna's recipe, eat them at home! Terrific dipped in ketchup and mustard.

1 egg
½ cup milk
1 cup Bisquick baking mix
2 tablespoons cornmeal
¼ teaspoon paprika
½ teaspoon dried mustard
⅛ teaspoon pepper
8-10 frankfurters
Vegetable oil for frying

Mix all ingredients together except wieners and oil. Dip wieners into batter and then fry in skillet in deep hot oil until brown on all sides. Drain.

Makes 4 servings.

RAYMONE'S BEANIE WEENIES

Ray Stevens' Beanie Weenies is a nice buffet dish for entertaining friends on a cold evening or even in the summer for around-the-campfire picnics.

1 medium onion, diced
1 medium green pepper, diced
1 cup diced celery
2 tablespoons butter
½ pound ground beef
1 55-ounce can baked beans
1 16-ounce package wieners
1 cup brown sugar
Tabasco

Saute the onion, green pepper and celery in butter until the onions look slightly opaque. Transfer this mixture to a large pot and set aside.

Crumble and brown ground beef. Drain grease and transfer meat to large pot, also. Drain baked beans, remove any pork fat, and add to large pot. Cut wieners into bite-size pieces and add to pot. Stir in brown sugar. Add Tabasco to taste — I like 15 dashes. Heat thoroughly over low temperature and serve.

Makes 8 to 12 servings.

THE WHITES' "ONE POT" JAMBALAYA

As the Cajuns of Louisiana say, "laissez le bon temps rouler!" or, "let the good times roll" . . . and they will with Sharon White's "One Pot" Jambalaya.

1   link (about 1 pound) smoked sausage, pork is best
1   2½ to 3 pound chicken, cut up (or chosen pieces)
    Salt and pepper
4   large onions, chopped
1   clove garlic, minced (optional)
5   cups water
3   cups long-cooking rice
2   teaspoons salt

Slice sausage in ½-inch thick slices and brown in a skillet (preferably an iron skillet.) Remove sausages, leaving grease in the skillet.

Salt and pepper chicken and brown it in the same skillet. Remove chicken, then add onions and saute in the same grease as sausage and chicken. Sprinkle with garlic, if desired. Return chicken and sausage to skillet with the onions and garlic. Add water and rice. Let mixture come to a full boil. Add salt. Turn heat to low, cover, and cook for 30 minutes or until rice is done. Don't remove lid until 30 minutes are up or the rice will be gummy. "If your rice appears gummy when you remove the lid, don't stir it for a while. The rice will dry out before you serve it."

Makes 6 to 8 servings.

LITTLE JIMMY DICKENS' PIGS AND TATERS

Jimmy's Pigs & Taters has a different twist than the usual. We suggest it for a light supper as well as lunch.

½   teaspoon onion juice
1   tablespoon minced parsley
1   egg yolk
2   cups mashed taters (potatoes)
    Salt and pepper to taste
6-8 small sausage links, cooked and drained
    Dry bread crumbs
1   whole egg, beaten and diluted with 2 tablespoons cold water
    Vegetable oil

Add onion juice, parsley and egg yolk to mashed potatoes. Season to taste with salt and pepper. Beat thoroughly.

Coat each sausage with potato mixture and shape into croquettes. Roll in bread crumbs, dip in diluted egg, then roll in crumbs again.

Place in skillet and fry in deep fat at 375 degrees until golden brown. Drain well.

Makes 6 to 8 croquettes.

TANYA TUCKER'S CHICKEN TAMALES

Tanya's friend, Dawn Warinner, makes this Mexican dish for Tanya. She loves it and asked that we include it.

2½-3 dozen corn husks
2½ 2½- to 3-ound chickens
3 pounds Monterey Jack cheese, shredded
16-20 jalapeno peppers
1 cup chopped black olives
4 cups masa flour
2 tablespoons salt
½ cup lard
 Drippings from chicken
 Chicken broth (optional)

Soak corn husks in water overnight.

Preheat oven to 350 degrees.

Roast chicken for 1 to 1½ hours. Cool. Pick meat from bone and shred. Reserve chicken drippings for the masa.

To make tamale filling, chop jalapenos and mix with cheese and chicken. Add black olives. Mix well. Set aside.

To make masa, mix flour and salt with lard and pan drippings from the chicken. Mix well until smooth, like a thin frosting. (Use chicken broth if mixture needs thinning.) Spread masa on corn husks to ¼-inch thickness. Place tamale filling in the middle. Roll husks and fold ends. Steam on a rack over hot water 1 to 1½ hours. Cool. Masa will firm even more as tamales cool.

Makes 2½ to 3 dozen.

KITTY WELLS' CHICKEN SAUTE CONTINENTAL

Kitty says, "I'm happiest when I can be in the kitchen. To me, the most fun in the world is to work for my family. I love to experiment with new and old recipes. This chicken dish is a family favorite."

2 quartered 3-pound chickens
2 teaspoons salt
 All-purpose flour for dredging
½ cup butter
¼ cup chopped onions
1 glove garlic, mashed
2 cups chicken broth
1 cup sliced fresh mushrooms
¼ teaspoon dried thyme
¼ teaspoon dried rosemary
2 cups canned tomatoes

Salt chicken and dredge in flour. In a large skillet, saute onion and garlic in butter. Add chicken and cook 12 minutes, turning occasionally.

In separate bowl, combine chicken broth, mushrooms, thyme, rosemary and tomatoes. Pour over the chicken in the skillet and continue to cook over medium heat for 20 minutes or until chicken is tender. Serve hot over steaming rice.

Makes 4 to 8 servings.

LEE GREENWOOD'S OVEN FRIED CHICKEN

Bake enough for 2 or 20! The amount of chicken used will determine the amount of the other ingredients.

Chicken parts
Crisco Shortening or vegetable oil
Egg, beaten
Salt and pepper
Dry bread crumbs

Preheat oven to 375 degrees.

Use leg and thigh quarters, or breast halves, of chicken. Wash and pat dry with paper towels. Roll in melted Crisco or oil. Dip in beaten egg. Season quickly with salt and pepper to taste before rolling chicken pieces in dry bread crumbs to coat both sides well.

Arrange pieces on a cooling rack placed on a greased cookie sheet. Bake for 45 minutes to 1 hour. A loose tent of foil placed over the chicken will hasten the baking process.

Serves any number desired, depending on amount of chicken used.

Editors Note: If using parts of one fryer, ½ cup oil, 1 egg and ¾ cup crumbs should be enough. The exact quantity of ingredients really depends on the size of the chicken.

ALABAMA'S QUICK-FRY CHICKEN AND VEGETABLES

Alabama drummer Mark Herndon enjoys Japanese food more than any other type of food, and he offers this stir-fried dish for your pleasure.

2	tablespoons vegetable oil
1	pound boneless, skinless chicken breasts, cut into ½-inch cubes
1	medium onion, chopped
1	medium green pepper, seeded and chopped
½	teaspoon minced fresh garlic
1	teaspoon salt
2	medium tomatoes, coarsely chopped
	Cooked rice

Heat oil in a medium skillet over medium heat. When oil is very hot, add chicken and stir and cook until golden brown on all sides, about 2 minutes. Add remaining ingredients except tomatoes. Cook 3 minutes more. Add tomatoes and stir until tomatoes are warmed through. Serve over cooked rice. Makes 4 servings.

CONWAY TWITTY'S TEXAS FRIED CHICKEN

Conway tells us that his Fried Chicken is a cousin to chicken fried steak, another Texas favorite. He says it's especially good for those who need a little help when it comes to frying chicken.

½ cup all-purpose flour
½ teaspoon salt
¼ teaspoon pepper
1 3-pound chicken, cut into serving pieces
1 egg, beaten
¼ cup milk
1½ cups fine bread crumbs or cracker crumbs, or mixture of both
¼ cup Crisco shortening (or butter, bacon grease or vegetable oil)
¼ cup chicken stock or water
1 8-ounce can pineapple rings

Mix together the flour, salt and pepper and sprinkle over all sides of the chicken. Mix together the egg and milk and dip the chicken first in this, then into the crumbs and cover well.

Preheat oven to 300 degrees.

Heat Crisco in a skillet until very hot. Brown the chicken on all sides. Add stock or water to the skillet. Cover the pan, place in the oven, and bake for 45 to 60 minutes. Serve with the sauce from the pan. If you prefer a thicker sauce, add a little flour to the drippings after removing the chicken and stir over low heat for a few minutes. Serve chicken with pineapple rings.

Makes 2 to 4 servings.

THE STATLER BROTHERS' BOXLEY STYLE CHICKEN

A wonderfully hearty dish with three kinds of meat and a creamy, mild sauce!

2 2½-ounce jars dried beef
1 pound bacon
8-10 chicken breast halves, boned and skinned
1 10¾-ounce can cream of chicken soup, undiluted
1 8-ounce carton sour cream

Preheat oven to 300 degrees.

Cover bottom of 9 by 13-inch baking dish evenly with dried beef. Wrap one bacon strip around each chicken breast half, and place wrapped chicken on top of dried beef in casserole dish.

Mix soup and sour cream together until smooth and spread on top of chicken breasts. Bake for 2½ hours, or until chicken is very tender.

Makes 8 to 10 servings.

GEORGE STRAIT'S KING RANCH CHICKEN

George grew up on a ranch and once roped a turkey! But we'll let George tell you about that — turn to page 154 while this recipe is cooking.

1   10¾-ounce can cream of chicken soup
1   10¾-ounce can cream of mushroom soup
¾   cup chicken broth
½   10-ounce can Ro-Tel tomatoes with green chile peppers
4   chicken breast halves, boned and skinned
1   11-ounce package corn tortillas cut into 6 pieces
1   medium onion, chopped
½   pound cheddar cheese, shredded

Preheat oven to 350 degrees.

Mix together the first 4 ingredients and set aside. In a greased 9 by 13-inch casserole, layer the ingredients in the following order: chicken, tortillas, onions, soup mixture and top with cheese. Bake for 1 hour or until mixture is bubbly.

Makes 6 servings.

T. G. SHEPPARD'S COOKED CHICKEN SANDWICHES

Terrific for lunch or a light supper.

1   8-ounce package uncooked crescent dinner rolls
1½   cup cooked chopped chicken
1   3-ounce package cream cheese, softened
2   tablespoons butter, softened
2   teaspoons chopped chives
2   tablespoons milk
     Salt and pepper to taste
3   tablespoons dried minced onions
4   tablespoons Italian-seasoned bread crumbs
4   teaspoons butter

Preheat oven to 375 degrees.

Separate rolls into 4 squares. Mix the remaining ingredients (with the exception of the bread crumbs and butter) and divide evenly on middle of each dough square. Roll dough around the mixture and pinch edges.

Place on a greased cookie sheet. Put Italian bread crumbs and a teaspoon of butter on top of each roll. Bake until the rolls are golden brown, about 15 to 20 minutes.

Makes 4 servings.

EMMYLOU HARRIS' CHICKEN ELEGANTÉ

Despite Emmylou's remark that she is "more at home in the woods with cornmeal, a campfire and an iron skillet," this is a delicious entree that is best made in the kitchen!

¼ cup butter or margarine
¼ cup all-purpose flour
¼ cup crumbled blue cheese
1 10¾-ounce can cream of mushroom soup, undiluted
2-3 cups diced chicken
½ cup Parmesan cheese
½ teaspoon dried marjoram
2 10-ounce packages frozen broccoli pieces
1 cup sour cream
¼ cup buttered bread crumbs

Preheat oven to 350 degrees.

Melt butter in pan, add flour, stir and let bubble for a few seconds. Add crumbled blue cheese and cream of mushroom soup, chicken, ¼ cup Parmesan cheese, marjoram and broccoli (broccoli pieces are better for this recipe than finely chopped broccoli.) Fold in sour cream.

Pour into casserole. Top with buttered bread crumbs and remaining ¼ cup Parmesan cheese and bake for about 30 minutes or until bubbly around edge.

Makes 6 servings.

Editors Note: Two bunches of fresh broccoli, with stems removed and blanched, may be substituted for frozen.

BILL ANDERSON'S CHICKEN AND BROCCOLI CASSEROLE

Curry makes this casserole, which is a nice main dish, particularly tasty.

4 chicken breast halves
1 tablespoon salt
1 10-ounce package frozen chopped broccoli
1 cup cream of mushroom soup, undiluted
1 cup mayonnaise
¼ teaspoon curry powder (optional)
Buttered cracker crumbs

Place chicken breasts in a 4-quart pan, cover with water, add salt; bring to a boil, then simmer 30 minutes or until tender. Drain and reserve broth for future use. Remove chicken from bones. Discard skin. Prepare broccoli according to package directions.

Preheat oven to 350 degrees.

Place chicken in 2-quart casserole. Mix soup, mayonnaise, curry powder and cooked broccoli in separate bowl. Pour over chicken. Top with crumbs. Bake for 20 to 30 minutes.

Makes 4 to 6 servings.

Editors Note: To make buttered cracker crumbs, melt 4 tablespoons butter in skillet and toss in 1 cup crushed crackers. One bunch cooked fresh broccoli may be substituted for frozen.

KITTY WELLS' CHICKEN AND DUMPLINGS

Kitty says, "One secret to dumpling making is rolling the dough very thin; another is not to stir the broth while the dumplings are cooking."

1   whole young hen, 3 to 4 pounds, cut up
3   tablespoons salt

Place chicken in a 6-quart pot and cover with water. Add salt. Boil until tender so chicken can be boned easily, about 1 hour. Remove chicken from broth, remove skin and bone. Cool broth and skim off fat.

To make dumplings:
1½   cups sifted all-purpose flour, slightly shaken down
     Dash salt
3   tablespoons cold vegetable shortening
7   tablespoons cold milk

Mix ingredients as for a pie crust. (Cut shortening into flour and salt and add milk until dough forms a ball.) Roll dough very thin, on a floured surface and cut into 1½ by 3-inch slices. Bring broth to a rolling boil and drop thin slices of dough into "volcanic boiling spots" one at a time. After last piece of dough is dropped in broth, allow to cook only about 6 minutes. Take pot off heat, add boned chicken, stir gently, then cover. (Might add a small dash of pepper to taste.) Let stand at least 1 hour before serving. Warm gently before serving.

Makes 4 servings.

THE STATLER BROTHERS' POPPY SEED CHICKEN

The poppy seeds on this chicken give a nice nutty taste.

4   chicken breast halves, boned and skinned
1   10¾-ounce can cream of chicken soup
1   8-ounce carton sour cream
2   tablespoons poppy seeds
35   Ritz crackers, crushed
6   tablespoons butter, melted

Preheat oven to 350 degrees.

Boil chicken in salted water to cover for 10 minutes. Cool and tear into bite-size pieces. In bowl, combine remaining ingredients. Add chicken. Pour into 2-quart baking dish. Cook for 1 hour.

Makes 2 to 4 servings.

THE WHITES' CHICKEN POT PIE

Cheryl White and her sister Sharon had plenty of lessons in the kitchen as children and used to always help "Mama" prepare dinner.

2   whole chicken breasts
     Salt and pepper
2   tablespoons all-purpose flour
     Water, enough to make a paste
     Other spices to suit your taste (nutmeg is nice)
1   10-ounce package frozen or 1 16-ounce can mixed vegetables
1   16-ounce can of veggies you like
     (or 1 additional package frozen vegetables)
     Crust for two-crust pie

Place chicken in pot and cover with water. Add salt and pepper. Boil chicken until tender. Remove from broth. Strain broth. Mix flour and water and add to broth to thicken. Add salt, pepper and spices to taste. Add vegetables to broth mixture. Simmer until thick.

Preheat oven to 350 degrees.

Meanwhile, remove chicken from bones. Remove skin. Put half the chicken and half the broth in each crust. Bake for 30 to 40 minutes.

This makes two pies. They wil freeze well baked or unbaked. When frozen unbaked, take from freezer, bake at 425 degrees for 20 minutes, then lower temperature to 350 degrees for an additional 30 to 40 minutes.

Makes 8 servings.

Editors Note: If you wish to use fresh vegetables, cut vegetables into small pieces, blanch and drain. Use 2 cups of cooked chopped vegetables.

LITTLE JIMMY DICKENS' MARINATED CHICKEN BREASTS

One of Little Jimmy Dickens' most requested recipes. He enjoys cooking, stating that he "finds that being creative in the kitchen is like creating music. In each case, I start with raw material and create something meaningful."

2   whole chicken breasts, boned and skinned
1   8-ounce can pineapple juice
½   cup Burgundy wine
½   cup soy sauce
1   teaspoon ginger

Place chicken in 9 by 9-inch baking dish. Mix together remaining ingredients and pour over chicken. Marinate 12 hours or overnight in the refrigerator.

Grill chicken over charcoal at medium heat, turning until desired tenderness and doneness, about 8 to 10 minutes per side.

Makes 2 to 4 servings.

THE OAK RIDGE BOYS'
BARBECUE CHICKEN A LA COCA-COLA

Truly an unusual barbecue chicken made with the ever-popular drink!

1   2½ to 3 pound chicken, cut up, salted and peppered
1   cup bottled barbecue sauce
1   cup Coca-Cola

Preheat oven to 325 degrees.

Place chicken in a 2-quart casserole dish. Mix barbecue sauce and Coca-Cola and pour over chicken. Bake for 55 minutes, or until chicken tests done.

Makes 4 servings.

THE STATLER BROTHERS' BARBECUED CHICKEN

"Barbecue" derives from the Mexican-Spanish "barbacoa," meaning to grill meat over a fire consisting of green wood. Today, barbecue means almost any type of cooking outdoors.

1   2½-3½ pound chicken, cut up
⅔   cup Bisquick baking mix
1½   teaspoons paprika
1¼   teaspoons salt
¼   teaspoon pepper

Mix Bisquick, paprika, salt and pepper; dredge chicken in mixture until well coated. Place chicken pieces, skin sides up, on hot grill about 5 inches over hot coals. Grill 20 minutes. Turn chicken; grill until done, about 10 to 15 minutes more.

Makes 6 servings.

CONWAY TWITTY'S MARINATED BARBECUED CHICKEN

Conway grills outside year-round. He says that "marinating the chicken for a good long while makes it special and well worth the advance planning."

¼   cup soy sauce
2   tablespoons pineapple juice
3   tablespoons sugar
5   ounces cooking sherry
6   whole chicken breasts

Mix together soy sauce, pineapple juice, sugar and sherry; add the chicken, cover, and place in the refrigerator for 24 hours. Cook outside on a low charcoal fire for 30 to 40 minutes, turning occasionally.

Makes 6 servings.

HANK WILLIAMS, JR.'S BAR-B-Q DEER CUBES

If using a regular charcoal grill rather than Hank's window screen and concrete block method, try placing a screen over the top of the grill so that the meat does not slip through the grates.

2   pounds deer meat, cut into 1-inch cubes
8   ounces barbecue sauce
1   12-ounce can beer

Mix all ingredients together. Make sure there is enough liquid to cover the meat. Marinate the meat for 24 hours. (This takes the wild taste out of the meat.) Drain meat well.

Slowly cook the deer cubes over hot charcoal or hickory chips on a window screen held up by concrete blocks. For added flavor, the leftover sauce can be used to brush over the cubes while they cook. Cook the meat to your desired degree of doneness, turning occasionally.

Makes 4 to 6 servings.

Editors Note: The meat of deer is often referred to as venison.

TAMMY WYNETTE'S CREAMED TUNA

Creamed tuna recipes have enjoyed enduring popularity. Try Tammy's for an easy and satisfying meal.

4   tablespoons butter-flavored Crisco
½   cup self-rising flour
2   cups milk
2   6½-ounce cans Bumble Bee white tuna, drained
4   hard cooked eggs, chopped
1   8½-ounce can LeSueur peas, drained
¼   teaspoon black pepper
      Salt to taste
      Toasted bread

Melt Crisco in large skillet. Add self-rising flour. Cook at medium, temperature until light brown. Add milk, stirring constantly until it reaches thick and desired consistency. Add tuna, eggs, peas and pepper; add salt. Simmer. Serve over toasted bread.

Makes 6 servings.

HELEN CORNELIUS' RAINBOW TROUT

Trout is freshwater fish, belonging to the same family as the salmon. Rainbow trout are indigenous to North America and available world-wide, as well as in Helen's kitchen.

6	8-ounce rainbow trout, cleaned
2	teaspoons salt
6	thin slices bacon
12	slices lemon
½	cup vegetable oil

Preheat oven to 350 degrees.

Wash trout thoroughly and sprinkle inside with 1½ teaspoons salt. Place one slice bacon and 2 slices lemon inside each. Use round toothpicks to hold in place.

Brush outside of trout with oil and sprinkle with the remaining salt. Wrap each fish loosely in foil. Bake for 35 to 40 minutes.

Serve with mixed green salad and cornbread.

Makes 6 servings.

DEBORAH ALLEN'S FLOUNDER

Fish is lauded as an important food due to its low cholesterol and calorie counts. Deborah's flounder adds a third reason for eating fish – taste!

2	2-pound flounder
1½	cups milk
½	cup butter, melted
¾	tablespoon poultry seasoning
	Salt and pepper
2	tablespoons lemon juice
1	tablespoon fresh minced parsley (dry may be substituted)
3	large green onions, diced, tops and bottoms
	Sliced lemon wedges (optional)

Preheat oven to 350 degrees.

Soak flounder in milk for 45 minutes. Place melted butter, poultry seasoning, salt, pepper and lemon juice in a baking dish. Add flounder. Top flounder with parsley and onions. Bake for 20 to 25 minutes or until fish flakes. Fish should be moist but flaky when done. Serve with sliced lemon wedges, if desired.

Makes 2 to 4 servings.

BRENDA LEE'S JAMBALAYA SHRIMP

In addition to being a Hank Williams song classic and an early hit for Brenda Lee, jambalaya has a wonderful story. Long ago, when New Orleans was under French rule, the proprietor of a small cafe received an unexpected guest. Desolate at having nothing fine enough to serve the distinguished visitor, the owner cried out to his cook, "Jean, balayez!" ("Blend together all you have!") The delighted guest loved the mixture and named it "Jean Balayez", later shortened to "Jambalaya."

1	pound fresh shrimp with shells
2	cups water
3	tablespoons lemon juice
1	tablespoon salt
1	cup diced cooked ham
¾	cup finely chopped onion
1	clove garlic, minced
2	tablespoons butter
3	cups quick meat broth (see note)
2	cups chopped tomatoes, sieved
2	tablespoons chopped parsley
1	teaspoon salt
¼	teaspoon dried thyme
⅛	teaspoon pepper
⅛	teaspoon cayenne pepper
⅛	teaspoon chili powder
½	bay leaf, crushed
1	cup raw rice

Wash shrimp in cold water. In large saucepan, combine water, lemon juice and salt. Bring to boil. Add shrimp. Cover tightly and simmer 5 minutes. Drain and cover shrimp with cold water to avoid further cooking. Drain. Remove shrimp legs and peel shells. Cut a slit along outer curved surface of shrimp to devein. Rinse shrimp quickly in cold water. Drain on absorbent paper and refrigerate until ready to use.

Combine ham, onion, and garlic. Heat butter in a saucepan over low heat. Add ham mixture, cover, and cook over medium heat until the onion is translucent. Add remaining ingredients. Blend well. Cover and bring to a boil. Uncover and add rice gradually, so boiling continues, stirring gently with a fork. Cover and simmer for 20 minutes or until rice kernel is entirely soft when pressed between your fingers. Add shrimp and simmer another 5 minutes. Serve "jambalaya" piping hot!

Makes 6 to 8 servings.

Editor's Note: With her busy schedule, Brenda does a "quick broth" thus: dissolve one beef bouillon cube (or ½ teaspoon concentrated meat extract) in one cup of hot water.

EDDY RAVEN'S SEAFOOD GUMBO

Eddy's Gumbo recipe is thick and rich with seafood as well as spicy with cayenne pepper and can be served as a first course, if you are hearty eaters.

1	cup vegetable oil
1	cup all-purpose flour
4	quarts water
2	pounds shrimp, peeled and deveined
1	pound fresh crabmeat (3 6½-ounce cans may be substitute if fresh cannot be found)
2	pints oysters
	Salt and cayenne pepper to taste
3	cups cooked rice
	Filé (optional)

In a large, heavy-bottomed pot, make a roux by heating oil and stirring in flour. Cook over medium heat, stirring constantly until a deep golden brown. Remove from heat. Add water gradually while stirring and return to heat. Bring to a boil, then reduce heat to low and cook from 2 to 3 hours, adding water when needed to maintain 4 quarts of liquid.

Add shrimp, crabmeat and oysters plus their liquor. Add salt and red pepper. Cook another 10 to 15 minutes. Serve in soup plates with ½ cup of hot cooked rice per serving. Use a dash of file in each plate, if desired.

Makes 6 servings.

Editors Note: File is a powder made from sassafras leaves and is used as a flavoring in gumbos. It is available in grocery and gourmet stores. Gumbo may be served as a main course or soup course.

BOBBY BARE'S OYSTER CASSEROLE

Of meals during his childhood, Bobby says, "All I remember is biscuits and gravy, beans and taters and cornbread, day in and day out ... now I eat anything I want, including oysters."

1	pint shucked oysters
¼	pound fresh mushrooms, sliced
2	tablespoons melted butter or margarine
1	10¾-ounce can cream of mushroom soup, undiluted
¾	cup oyster crackers
¼	cup grated Parmesan cheese
¼	cup cooking sherry
	Saltine cracker crumbs
	Butter

Preheat oven to 350 degrees.

Drain oysters and set aside. Saute mushrooms in butter or margarine; add mushroom soup, oyster crackers, cheese, cooking sherry and oysters. Mix well.

Spoon into a lightly greased 1½-quart casserole dish. Top with cracker crumbs, and dot with butter. Bake for about 30 minutes, or until bubbly.

Makes 4 servings.

BOBBY BARE'S WILD RICE AND SHRIMP

*A delicious treat. And easy too.
Try it!*

1   6-ounce package long grain wild rice
1   cup shredded Longhorn cheese
1   pound raw shrimp, shelled
1   cup cream of mushroom soup, undiluted
2   tablespoons minced onion
2   tablespoons butter
2   tablespoons lemon juice
1½   teaspoons Worcestershire sauce
½   teaspoon dry mustard
¼   teaspoon pepper
     Milk, if needed

Cook rice until tender, according to package directions.

Preheat oven to 375 degrees.

Put ½ cup cheese and all other ingredients in large bowl and mix well. Pour all of this mixture into a 2½-quart baking dish. If mixture is too thick, add a little milk and stir. Top with remaining cheese. Bake for 45 minutes.

Makes 4 to 6 servings.

T. G. SHEPPARD'S CHICKEN-SHRIMP SUPREME

*T. G. assures us that this recipe
from his wife Diana will elicit a
favorable response.*

4   tablespoons butter
½   pound fresh mushrooms, sliced
2   tablespoons sliced green onion
2   10¾-ounce cans cream of chicken soup, undiluted
½   cup sherry
½   cup half-and-half
1   cup shredded cheddar cheese
2   cups diced cooked chicken
2   cups cooked shrimp, shelled and deveined
2   tablespoons chopped parsley
     Hot buttered rice

In a 3-quart saucepan, melt butter; add mushrooms and onion and saute for 5 minutes. Add soup, and gradually stir in sherry and cream. Add cheese and cook over low heat, stirring occasionally, until cheese is melted. Add chicken and shrimp. Heat to serving temperature, but do not boil. Just before serving, stir in parsley.

Serve over rice, cooked according to package directions.

Makes 6 servings.

Louisiana prides itself on its special blends of food and music. Native Louisianan Eddy Raven has a deep appreciation for both. "Down in Louisiana," he notes, "there's such a mixture of music that you can't help but be influenced by it." And he has been: his recent #1 hit, "I Got Mexico," was a savory blend of country and reggae, reminiscent in a gentle way of the music that Cajuns have been cooking up for decades.

Louisiana's hold on Eddy is just as strong in the kitchen. His favorite meal is a toss-up between a full-course, Louisiana-style seafood dinner with shrimp, oysters and crab meat or a crawfish dinner. That is, unless the meal is breakfast. Then Eddy's got to have his grits.

Does he like to cook? "Not as much as I like to eat!" he says. The person whose cooking he enjoys the most is his wife, Gayle.

Eddy was born in Lafayette, the oldest of ten children. "The table was always crowded and noisy," he remembers. "And I always looked forward to Mama's fried chicken on Sundays." In a family that big, it's rare that each child eats his fill. No wonder that to this day, Eddy says he loves turkey during the holidays, mostly "because there's a lot of it."

For most of his career, Eddy was known primarily as a songwriter, penning hits for Don Gibson, Roy Clark, Jerry Reed, Roy Acuff ("Back in the Country") and the Oak Ridge Boys ("Thank God for Kids"). In the past couple of years, he has had Top Twenty hits of his own with "I Should've Called," "A Little Bit Crazy" and "She's Gonna Win Your Heart."

Writing hits for the stars and becoming one himself have made Eddy used to rubbing elbows with some famous folks. He's even getting used to having his head rubbed, too, which is what happened when he met Colonel Tom Parker, Elvis Presley's former manager. It seems the Colonel took such a shine to Eddy that he made a special point of rubbing Eddy's head for good luck. It certainly didn't hurt Eddy. A year later "I Got Mexico" became his first #1 record.

Meals with the rich and famous haven't been quite as eventful, but they have been just as memorable in their own way, says Eddy. "I've had a few good meals with some neat folks," he says, "but breakfast with Slim Pickens in Austin at the Driscoll Hotel during the filming of *Honeysuckle Rose* was the best." As for his worst meal, Eddy has a ready response: "How about refried chicken at a truckstop that will go un-named." We are happy to say that Eddy did not include the recipe here. Those he did include, the singer says, "are my favorites . . . old recipes I grew up with in Louisiana."

Eddy Raven

Jerry Reed

Jerry Reed is well-known for his talent as a guitar player, songwriter and actor. He is the first to admit, though, that his talent does not extend to the kitchen. He doesn't like to cook "because I really don't know how." In fact, he claims that the first time he ever tried to cook, "I was boiling water and I burnt it!" Luckily his wife, Prissy (short for Priscilla), is a very good cook who makes sure that Jerry doesn't have to fend for himself in the kitchen.

It was food that brought Jerry and Prissy together over 25 years ago. "It was outside Atlanta at a park where they had country music shows," Jerry recalls. "She had come out there with her parents and they had brought a lunch and I made 'em feed me." Today, Jerry says Prissy's his favorite cook.

His favorite meal is "good old Southern cooking": meat loaf, dried beans, fried okra, fried corn, mashed potatoes, sliced onions and iced tea. It's the kind of meal that Jerry grew up on as a child in Atlanta, except now there's a lot more food on the table. "I didn't have everything I wanted when I was a kid, but I had enough. My folks were from the cotton mill, so we never had a bunch of money. But we always had beans and 'taters when I needed beans and 'taters. It was a good life."

When Jerry was seven, his mother used the family's hard-earned money to buy her son a second-hand guitar for seven dollars. It turned out to be a wise investment. At ten, Jerry won a local talent contest. Eight years later, he was working for Capitol Records — writing songs, playing guitar on tour for stars like Ernest Tubb and trying to record hits of his own.

After a two-year hitch in the Army (where he had his worst and most memorable meal the first time he ate Army food), Jerry returned to music as a studio picker. But solo stardom eluded him until he met Chet Atkins, who became Jerry's producer. Elvis Presley soon recorded Jerry's "Guitar Man" and "U.S. Male." Jerry also scored with country hits of his own: "Amos Moses," "When You're Hot, You're Hot" and "Lord, Mr. Ford."

Atkins also helped Jerry get his start in front of the camera by introducing him to Glen Campbell. For two years, Jerry starred on "The Glen Campbell Goodtime Hour." Burt Reynolds invited Jerry to be in his movie *W.W. and the Dixie Dance Kings*. Since then, Jerry has starred in several movies and made numerous TV appearances. In 1985, he made his directing debut with *What Comes Around*.

Jerry hasn't "gone Hollywood" in his daily life. On tour he eats "whatever the nearest truck stop has to offer." He and Prissy still live on a 47-acre spread outside Nashville with their teenage daughter, Lottie. (Their other daughter, Seidina, is married.) Asked if he would consider moving to L.A., Jerry says, "No thank you. You can't get turnip greens out there, so I ain't leavin'."

Kenny Rogers

Kenny Rogers enjoys a hearty meal. "If you want to see a feast," he confesses, "take someone like me who spends so much time eating junk food out on the road and turn me loose ordering up a special holiday menu. There's no stopping the food!"

Kenny never takes his square meals for granted, though. He grew up the fourth of eight children born to a shipyard carpenter and a practical nurse. They all lived in a Houston federal housing project on $35 a month. Food was precious. "I remember what hunger is," he says. "We always had something to eat, but not always enough." It was a special treat, then, when the Rogers family went to visit Kenny's grandmother. There they received not only love and hospitality, but good cooking, too. "She was two-thirds Cherokee and the sweetest old lady, I'm telling you," says Kenny. "We would drive up to Apple Springs, Texas, where they lived, get in at 2 am, and my grandmother would get up, start the stove, and whip up biscuits — real biscuits — puffed up three and four inches high. I always loved going up there."

With memories of his own hardships firmly in mind, Kenny asked that fans bring cans of food to each of his shows during his concert tour of 1984. The cans were distributed to the needy through local relief agencies. The operation brought in well over a million pounds of canned goods. Not many stars could have influenced so many fans to do so much good so easily. But there is no denying Kenny's popularity. Eleven of his albums have gone platinum — the most ever by any artist. Among his biggest hits are "The Gambler," "Lucille," "Lady," and "She Believes in Me." He's also starred on the big screen and on TV.

When he's not working, Kenny relaxes with his wife, Marianne, and their young son, Christopher Cody. He admits that he's not much for cooking, but he does have one dish that he likes to fix: his Country Chicken Salad. "Growing up in Texas, I ate a lot of chicken," he says. "My mom knew more ways to fix chicken than anybody. Marianne's family ate a lot of chicken, too. Chicken and chicken salad were part of our childhood, and your childhood experiences stick with you. When Marianne and I met, we each had made our own recipes for chicken salad that we'd carried with us for years. We combined them into this recipe.

"If I'm home alone and hungry, this is about the most elaborate dish that I'll make," he says. "I think it's a practical and tasty way to express myself in the kitchen. I know it's filled with lots of good ingredients, and I have to admit, I sure do like the way it tastes."

T.G. Sheppard

T.G. Sheppard is a real believer in down home Southern cooking, even if he doesn't have an opportunity to do much of it himself. "I like to 'try' to cook," he says, "but I am so busy that I rarely have the time." Because he's frequently on tour, his meals are catch-as-catch-can. That means mostly "junk food and midway food at the fairs," he admits, "only because it's so convenient."

But when he does have the time, he loves to dig in to wife Diana's cooking, especially her "Southern-cooked vegetables, like black-eyed peas, fried okra, corn-on-the-cob, cornbread and sliced summer *homegrown* tomatoes." His favorite for holiday meals is just as Southern: "Turkey and dressing, cranberry sauce, layered salad, broccoli casserole, creamed sweet potatoes, hot rolls, Coca-Cola cake and baked custard. I love to eat during the holidays — mainly sweets, but I pay for it afterward and always have to diet."

T.G. Sheppard dieting? Most of his female fans (and he has plenty) would never believe it, and even if they did, they wouldn't care. They love him just the way he is. For the past ten years, he has consistently charmed them with chart-topping, heart-throbbing hits (at one time, 15 #1 singles in a row).

T.G. grew up in Humboldt, Tennessee, but took off for Memphis at age 16. He didn't miss small town life, but he did miss his mama's biscuit pudding, a dessert passed down from his great-great-grandmother. "I still love it," he says. "And she prepares it every time I visit."

In Memphis, T.G. became good friends with Elvis Presley, who gave him a diamond ring that he wears to this day. T.G. says his most memorable meal was just hamburgers with Elvis at the Memphis Theatre. A close second was the dinner he had with Burt Reynolds at the Stockyard Restaurant in Nashville. T.G. remembers a meal of vegetable soup, salad, steak, stuffed baked potatoes, iced tea and good company.

One meal that T.G. would rather forget took place in Mexico, where he sampled one of the local delicacies. "It was goat meat," he recalls all too vividly. "Ugh! I came down with a severe case of food poisoning." Rest assured: the recipes included here, says T.G., are "recipes that Diana cooks that I especially like."

Ricky Skaggs

Ricky Skaggs is "as good as chicken fried steak," says Emmylou Harris. "I'm as country as corn bread," is the way Ricky puts it. And it shows, right down to his favorite meal — fried catfish, pinto beans and fried corn bread. He enjoys fixing meals himself, but he'd rather eat his mother's cooking. "We used to butcher a hog every winter," he recalls. "For days, Mother would fix tenderloin, hot biscuits and gravy. There ain't nothing like it."

Memories of good Southern cooking are not the only things Ricky has brought with him from his childhood. "Growing up in a mountain environment (Cordell, Kentucky) was real important to me, and it comes out in all the music I do," says Ricky.

The music started coming out of Ricky early, and when it came, it was Kentucky bluegrass. When Ricky was just five, his father bought him a mandolin, the instrument of bluegrass pioneer Bill Monroe. Within two weeks, the youngster had taught himself to play and sing along. By age ten, he'd mastered the guitar and fiddle, as well. Ricky honed his talent with the Clinch Mountain Boys bluegrass band and several other bands until, at the ripe old age of 23, he met Emmylou Harris. She invited him to join her Hot Band, where he soon impressed a whole new audience with his instrumental virtuosity and his pure, mountain tenor.

Since going solo in 1980, Ricky has managed to do the impossible, pleasing traditionalists with his bluegrass roots while winning new converts with more modern country stylings. In 1982, he was voted the CMA Male Vocalist of the Year, and at age 27, he was added to the roster of the Grand Ole Opry — the youngest person ever granted that honor. He was voted the CMA Entertainer of the Year for 1985.

With his mountain roots, Ricky's a family man, through and through. Even though he once ate a lunch of fried chicken, cabbage and soup beans with hero Bill Monroe, Ricky insists his most memorable meal took place at home on Christmas Eve, 1984, when he was with his wife Sharon (of the singing White family), his children and his folks. For Ricky, holiday meals could consist of pinto beans and fried corn bread, "anything," he says, "as long as it's with Sharon and the children."

Every Fourth of July since 1969, the Statlers have given a concert in their hometown of Staunton, Virginia. "It's a town of about 22,000," says lead singer Don Reid, "but the last time, 74,000 people showed up."

"I know," says his brother Harold, the bass singer and chief cut-up of the group. "We had them all over to my place for dinner."

"You did?" says Don doubtfully.

"Yeah. We have a biiiiiig table, but we still had to take turns eating." Pause. "We only had silverware for 73,000."

The Statlers have a long-standing reputation for goodhearted humor, down-home values and distinctive singing. That reputation goes back to at least 20 years to 1965, when they went straight to the top with their first hit, the Grammy-winning "Flowers on the Wall."

What has kept the Statlers at it for so long? Well, it can't be just the Dr. Peppers that they're known to be so fond of. Or the candy bars they like to munch while on their tour bus. Harold Reid has his own explanation: "Greed," he jokes. "We work awfully hard to keep from starving; we'll do anything to keep from getting to work at a real job." Harold may joke about the Statlers not bringing home the bacon legitimately, but their fans know better. Hits like "Bed of Roses," "The Class of '57," and "Elizabeth" didn't just drop into the laps of Don, Harold, baritone Phil Balsley, and tenor Jimmy Fortune.

It's hard to believe it now, but when they were starting out, the Statlers took their name from a hotel box of Statler Tissues. "We could just as easily have been the Kleenex Brothers," they like to joke.

The spotlight hasn't changed the Statlers, though. They are still family men, content to live in sleepy Staunton, where their old elementary school building, now renovated, serves as their headquarters. Harold Reid resides on a 15-acre farm near Staunton with his wife, Brenda. They have a son and four daughters. Don Reid is a member of the Board of Directors of the Staunton YMCA, and elder of Olivet Presbyterian Church and coach of a Little League baseball team. He and his wife, Gloria, have two sons. Phil Balsley keeps track of the group's business affairs and is also a member of the choir at Olivet Church. He and his wife, Wilma, have three children. Jimmy Fortune, who replaced the retired Lew DeWitt in 1982, was born 40 miles away from Staunton, but he has also settled there with wife Carole and their two children. "Staunton is our hometown," Don explains, "and it's a blessing now to be able to come back to it from touring and slip back easily into normal life."

Normal on most days, that is. Of course, dinner on the Fourth of July will always be a little unusual for everybody in Staunton, as long as the Statlers have anything to say about it.

The Statler Brothers

Ray Stevens

Ray Stevens is a man of many tastes and many moods. As a songwriter and singer he's been responsible for some very silly songs, "Ahab the Arab," "Guitarzan" and some rather thoughtful ones as well, "Mr. Businessman" and "Everything Is Beautiful." His eating habits are just as varied: he says his favorite food is Italian pasta dishes, but he admits that when he's on the road he eats mostly hamburgers. And he's also a big fan of seafood; in fact, his favorite restaurant meal is "boiled shrimp over linguine noodles with lemon-butter sauce and salad." It's funny that Ray can be a big fan of sophisticated dishes like pasta and seafood, and yet spend alot of his time eating hamburgers. But then Ray Stevens is. . . well. . .a funny kind of guy.

He's certainly not an easy artist to classify. He's probably best known for two very different records: "The Streak," which sold 5 million copies in 1974 at the height of that bizarre national fad, and "Everything Is Beautiful," which won him a Grammy Award in 1970. In 1975 he also won a Grammy for another surprising creation: his bluegrass arrangement of the Errol Garner classic "Misty."

Ray's eclectic tastes developed very early during his youth in his hometown of Clarkdale, Georgia, located about 20 miles north of Atlanta. There he began taking piano lessons at the age of six. Around the same time, he started spending his summers at a local swimming pool, where there was a jukebox that played all the popular country music stars – Lefty Frizzell, Ernest Tubb, Eddy Arnold. When he was 10, Ray moved with his family to Albany, Georgia, where Ray was quickly introduced to a new kind of music – the rhythm and blues sounds of Ray Charles, Fats Domino, the Coasters, and the Drifters. In high school, Ray formed his own r&b band, which soon was playing local nightclubs and dances. But it seems that Ray just couldn't get enough of the spotlight, because in between sets he performed as a stand-up comedian.

Ray went on to college at Georgia State, where he majored in classical piano and musical theory, but he continued performing, often with another future star – his friend Jerry Reed. In 1961, Ray moved to Nashville, starting out as a production assistant at Mercury Records. He didn't stay behind the scenes for long. He had his first novelty hit that year, and it was a mouthful: "Jeremiah Peabody's Poly-unsaturated Quick-dissolving Fast-acting Pleasant-tasting Green and Purple Pills." He followed that up with two comedy smashes – "Ahab the Arab" and "Harry the Hairy Ape" – and he was on his way. In between the successes of his own records, he also managed to arranged and produce records for Dolly Parton, Brenda Lee, Charlie Rich, Chet Atkins, and others.

Nowadays, when he's not concocting new songs and recordings, Ray likes to do a little cooking in the kitchen. He finds that "it's very creative." But he has an even more important reason for his interest in cooking: "I like to eat," he admits. His favorite cook of all, though, is his mother. He may eat a lot of hamburgers today, but he looks back fondly at those home-cooked meals that were mostly vegetables.

As in everything else, Ray has given this cookbook his all: these recipes, he says, "are the only ones I had!"

George Strait

When George Strait wants beef, he knows how to get some in a hurry. "Roping steers is one of my favorite hobbies," he explains. "Whenever I have any spare time, I'll practice with some friends or do some jackpot (contest) roping."

Born in Poteet, Texas and raised in nearby Pearsall, George grew up learning to rope and ride. When George's grandfather died, his father took over operation of the family's 2000-acre cattle ranch in Big Wells, Texas. During the week, young George and his older brother attended school; on weekends, they'd rope and ride and tend the family's cattle ranch.

Country music didn't figure prominently in George's life until he joined the Army. There he taught himself to play guitar on an old beat-up instrument with the aid of some Hank Williams songbooks. Eventually his playing and especially his singing earned him a place in an Army country band put together by his commanding officer. George spent the last year of his tour of duty just playing in the band, honing his talent. Afterwards, he enrolled at Southwest Texas University and graduated in 1979 with a degree in agricultural education. After graduation he managed a cattle ranch outside of San Marcos, Texas full-time — during the days. At night, he sang with his Ace in the Hole Band, whose members he'd met in college.

It was not an easy life. "Ranching isn't nine-to-five," he explains. "It's more like sunup to sundown. I'd have about half an hour to get cleaned up and get to the night's gig." Three years of that turned him sour on the music business. He was about to give up singing when his wife, Norma, got him to give it one more try. It worked. In the last four years, George has recorded several hits, including "Fool-Hearted Memory" and "Amarillo by Morning."

"Singin' is a whole lot easier than ropin' cattle," George admits. "I never was all that great at ropin'. I just enjoyed doing it. It takes a lot of time away from my family, so I kinda put ropin' on the back burner for now. I also like to hunt during hunting season," he says. "Lately we've been going bass fishing a lot, too."

When it comes to holiday meals, George knows how to catch that kind of entrée, too. "I don't even know how that story got around Nashville," he says, "but, yes, I did rope a turkey once. I was checking some cattle and we were near a 700-acre field planted to oats. There was this big ol' tom turkey there all by himself. I wasn't gonna mess with him, but then he flew across the fence and I caught him running down the fence line. I roped at him a couple of times and eventually got off my horse and roped him. Then I didn't know what to do with him." Eventually, George says, he let the turkey go, because it wasn't the holiday season and the Mexican recipes he loves don't call for turkey.

Desserts and Drinks

MINNIE PEARL'S CHESS CAKE

To make sure your egg whites beat up nice and stiff have your bowl and beaters very clean and dry!

1	cup butter or margarine
1	pound box confectioners' sugar
1	cup sugar
4	egg yolks, beaten
2	cups sifted all-purpose flour
2	teaspoons baking powder
¼	teaspoon salt
1	cup chopped pecans
4	egg whites
1	teaspoon vanilla

Preheat oven to 325 degrees. Lightly grease a 9 by 13-inch pan.

Melt butter and cool slightly. Add sugars and egg yolks to butter. Sift flour, baking powder and salt together. Stir into egg and butter mixture. Stir in pecans.

Beat egg whites until stiff. Add vanilla. Fold whites into batter. Pour batter into pan. Bake for 30 to 45 minutes or until done. Cool on wire rack and cut into squares.

Makes 18 squares.

THE OAK RIDGE BOYS' RAISIN PECAN CAKE TOPPING

A favorite recipe of William Lee Golden of the Oak Ridge Boys, often made by his mother.

½	16-ounce box seedless raisins, washed and drained
2	cups shelled pecans
¾	cup water
1½	cups sugar
1	teaspoon vanilla

Prepare your favorite three-layer yellow cake.

Grind up raisins and pecans in a grinder or food processor. In a saucepan, bring water and sugar to a boil. Add ground raisins, pecans and vanilla. Spread mixture between layers of three-layer yellow cake. Ice top of cake but not sides.

Makes topping for one cake.

Editors Note: See editors' note on Bill Anderson's Hummingbird Cake.

T. G. SHEPPARD'S COCA-COLA CAKE

Recipes for Coca-Cola Cake appear in many cookbooks, especially Southern ones, but we think this one by T. G. Sheppard is unusually good.

2	cups all-purpose flour
2	cups sugar
1	cup butter
3	tablespoons cocoa
1	cup Coca-Cola
1	teaspoon baking soda
½	cup buttermilk
2	eggs, beaten
1	teaspoon vanilla
2	cups miniature marshmallows

Preheat oven to 350 degrees.

Combine flour and sugar in bowl. In a saucepan, melt butter, add cocoa and Coca-Cola; heat until just boiling. Cool slightly. Pour over flour and sugar. Stir until blended. Dissolve baking soda in buttermilk and gradually add to flour mixture, along with eggs and vanilla. Mix well.

Stir in marshmallows and pour into greased and floured 9 by 13-inch baking pan. This will be a thin batter, and marshmallows will come to the top. Bake for 35 to 40 minutes. Ice while hot.

Icing

½	cup butter
3	tablespoons cocoa
6	tablespoons Coca-Cola
1	pound box confectioners' sugar
1	teaspoon vanilla
1	cup chopped nuts

Combine butter, cocoa and Coca-Cola in saucepan. Heat until boiling. Pour over sugar in electric mixer bowl. Beat until smooth. Add vanilla. Stir in nuts and pour over the hot cake.

Makes 8 servings.

THE STATLER BROTHERS' MOUNTAIN POUND CAKE

Something the Statler Brothers wouldn't miss taking on the road when they're touring. Now you can enjoy it at home.

1   cup butter, softened
½   cup Crisco (Crisco only)
3   cups sugar
5   eggs
3   cups all-purpose flour
1   cup milk
½   teaspoon baking powder
1½   teaspoons vanilla
½   teaspoon lemon juice (optional)

Cream butter, Crisco and sugar. Mix in eggs one at a time. Stir in flour and milk alternately, and add baking powder with the last of the flour. Add vanilla and lemon juice.

Pour into a greased and floured 10-inch tube pan. Place in a cold oven. Turn oven to 350 degrees. Bake 1 hour and 15 minutes. DO NOT OPEN THE OVEN DOOR – EVEN ONCE. Remove from oven and let stand on rack to cool completely before removing from pan.

Makes 8 to 10 servings.

TAMMY WYNETTE'S SOUR CREAM POUND CAKE

Serve with fresh fruit and whipped cream, ice cream or just plain.

1   cup butter-flavored Crisco
3   cups sugar
6   eggs
1   cup sour cream
3   cups all-purpose flour
¼   teaspoon baking soda
¼   teaspoon salt
2   teaspoons vanilla or coconut flavoring

Preheat oven to 325 degrees.

In mixing bowl, cream Crisco and sugar thoroughly. Add eggs, beating after each one. Blend remaining ingredients alternately, beating thoroughly after each addition. Pour batter into greased and floured 10-inch tube pan. Bake for approximately 1 hour. Cool on wire rack. Remove from pan.

Makes 8 to 10 servings.

KITTY WELLS' 7-UP POUND CAKE

7-Up in pound cake? Kitty's been cooking for a long time and she promises this cake is great!

1½ cups butter, softened
3   cups sugar
5   eggs
1   cup 7-Up
3   cups all-purpose flour
1   teaspoon lemon juice
1   teaspoon vanilla

Preheat oven to 350 degrees.

In large bowl, cream butter and sugar. Add eggs, one at a time, beating well after each. Add flour and 7-Up alternately, mixing well after each addition. Fold in lemon juice and vanilla. Bake in greased and floured 10-inch tube pan for 1 hour and 15 minutes. Cool on wire rack and remove from pan.

Makes 8 to 10 servings.

CHARLIE DANIELS' GREAT CHOCOLATE CAKE

Mrs. Charlie Daniels assures us that "this is a simple cake and I always have good luck with it. It's Charlie's and little Charlie's favorite!"

1   cup butter or margarine, softened
2   cups sugar
2   eggs
1   teaspoon vanilla
3   cups sifted all-purpose flour
½   cup cocoa
2   teaspoons baking soda
1   teaspoon salt
2   cups buttermilk

Preheat oven to 350 degrees.

Grease and flour 2 8-inch round layer cake pans or one large sheet cake pan. Cream butter and gradually beat in sugar until fluffy. Add one egg at a time and beat well after each, about 2 minutes. Add vanilla. Add sifted dry ingredients alternately with buttermilk using low speed of mixer to beat. Pour into pans.

Bake for 35 to 40 minutes. Remove from pans after a few minutes on rack and cool. Frost with Chocolate Butter Frosting.

Frosting
1   1-pound box confectioners' sugar
½   cup cocoa
⅛   teaspoon salt
½   cup soft butter or margarine
1   teaspoon vanilla
5-7 tablespoons milk

To make frosting, mix all ingredients together and beat on low speed until smooth. Spread on bottom of each cooled layer, press bottoms together and frost the top and sides. This icing tastes best after it sits on cake for about 1 hour.

Makes 8 to 10 servings.

THE WHITES' CHOCOLATE CAKE

Buck White's Aunt Kathryn baked this for her five boys and Buck's wife, Patty, bakes it for their four girls. Son-in-law Ricky Skaggs likes it, too! It's obviously a family hit.

2½	cups sugar
1	cup Crisco
2	eggs
1	cup buttermilk
2	teaspoons baking soda
2½	cups all-purpose flour
¼	cup cocoa
½	teaspoon salt
1	teaspoon vanilla
1	cup boiling water

Preheat oven to 350 degrees.

In a large bowl, mix sugar, Crisco and eggs. Put soda in buttermilk and stir. Add to sugar, Crisco and egg mixture. Mix well. Add flour, cocoa and salt. Stir in vanilla and boiling water. Place in 9 by 13-inch greased and floured pan and bake for 40 minutes. Frost while warm.

Frosting

2	tablespoons cocoa
2	cups sugar
½	cup milk
½	cup margarine
¼	teaspoon salt
1	teaspoon vanilla

Mix all ingredients except vanilla in a saucepan and bring to a boil, stirring well. Cook until a drop of mixture forms a soft ball in cold water. Then boil 2 minutes longer. Add vanilla and beat until mixture is cool enough to spread on warm cake.

Makes 16 servings.

CONWAY TWITTY'S MISSISSIPPI MUD CAKE

"Easy to throw together, really tasty and a famous Southern specialty. When it cooks, the top cracks open, making it look like Delta soil baking in the summer heat," says Conway.

2	cups sugar
1	cup Crisco shortening
4	eggs
1½	cups all-purpose flour
⅓	cup cocoa
¼	teaspoon salt
1	tablespoon vanilla
1	cup finely chopped pecans

Preheat oven to 350 degrees.

Cream sugar and Crisco. Add eggs and beat well. Add flour, cocoa and salt and beat well. Stir in vanilla and nuts. Beat the mixture thoroughly. Pour into a greased 9 x 13 inch baking pan and bake for 25 minutes. Remove from oven and cool on wire rack.

Icing

⅓	cup cocoa
1	pound confectioners' sugar
1	cup margarine, melted
1	teaspoon vanilla
1	cup finely chopped pecans

In a medium-size bowl, sift together the cocoa and confectioners' sugar. Add melted margarine, vanilla and pecans. Beat together by hand and pour over the cake.

Makes 8 to 10 servings.

BILL ANDERSON'S HUMMINGBIRD CAKE

Fruity, nutty and sweet. A nice dessert with coffee if having friends over.

3	cups cake flour
2	cups sugar
1	teaspoon salt
1	teaspoon baking soda
1	teaspoon cinnamon
3	eggs, beaten
1½	cups vegetable oil
1½	teaspoons vanilla
1	8-ounce can crushed pineapple, undrained
2	cups mashed bananas
1	cup chopped pecans

Preheat oven to 350 degrees.

Mix dry ingredients. Add eggs and oil. Stir until flour is moistened – do not beat. Stir in vanilla, pineapple, banana and 1 cup nuts. Spoon into 3 9-inch round greased and floured cake pans. Bake for 25 to 30 minutes. Cool in pans 10 minutes, then turn out.

Frosting:

2	8-ounce packages cream cheese, softened
1	cup margarine, softened
2	16-ounce boxes powdered sugar
2	teaspoons vanilla
	Dab of milk, if needed
1	cup chopped pecans

Mix cream cheese, margarine, sugar and vanilla. Add milk if too thick. Spread icing between layers of cake and on top and sides. Sprinkle nuts on top.

Makes 8 servings.

Editors Note: To have layers stack evenly, put 2 bottoms together and slice small amount off top of second layer, if uneven, so third layer will sit evenly.

TANYA TUCKER'S ITALIAN CREAM CAKE

"My mother is the greatest cook in the world," Tanya says. "Next to her, I love to watch the Galloping Gourmet on television. Whether he knows it or not, we run around our separate kitchens together quite a bit."

½	cup butter or margarine, softened
½	cup vegetable shortening
2	cups sugar
5	egg yolks
2	cups all-purpose flour
1	teaspoon baking soda
1	cup buttermilk
1	teaspoon vanilla
1	3½-ounce can of shredded coconut
5	egg whites, beaten stiff
1	cup chopped pecans

Preheat oven to 350 degrees.

Cream butter and shortening together in bowl; add sugar and beat. Add egg yolks and beat. Combine flour and baking soda; add to creamed mixture, alternately with buttermilk. Add vanilla, coconut and chopped pecans. Mix well. Fold in egg whites; bake in 3 greased and floured 8-inch round cake pans for 25 minutes. Cool on wire racks.

Icing:

8	ounces cream cheese, softened
1	1-pound box confectioners' sugar
½	cup butter or margarine, softened
1	teaspoon vanilla
½	cup chopped pecans

Place all ingredients except pecans in a bowl and beat until smooth and creamy. Stir in pecans. Spread icing between each layer of cake, and on top and sides.

Makes 10 to 12 servings.

BILL ANDERSON'S FAVORITE FRUIT CAKE

A hint from Bill: "After this cake has been baked, keep it fresh and moist by cutting up half an apple and placing the pieces in the cake's center hole. Change the apple pieces every two to three days."

½	cup butter, softened
1¼	cups sugar
5	eggs, separated
1¼	cups all-purpose flour
1	heaping teaspoon baking powder
1	teaspoon salt
1	lemon, juice and grated rind
1	teaspoon vanilla
3	8-ounce boxes pitted dates, diced
3	slices candied pineapple, diced
¾	pound candied cherries, halved
4	cups shelled pecan pieces

Preheat oven to 300 degrees.

Cream butter and sugar. Beat egg yolks in separate bowl and add to butter and sugar. Combine flour, baking powder and salt. Divide in half. Fold one half into egg mixture alternately with lemon juice and grated rind and vanilla.

Add other half of the flour to fruit and nuts and mix well. Beat egg whites until stiff. Fold egg whites into batter and mix gently. ("I mix with my hands.") Pour batter into a 10-inch tube pan lined with brown paper and well greased. Bake for 2 to 2½ hours or until cake tester comes out clean. Cool on wire rack. Remove from pan and serve.

Makes 10 to 12 servings.

THE STATLER BROTHERS' CARROT CAKE

As anyone who's ever had carrot cake knows, this recipe tastes nothing like carrots. It's rich, sweet and easy to make!

2	cups all-purpose flour
2	cups sugar
2	teaspoons baking soda
2½	teaspoons cinnamon
1½	cups Wesson or other vegetable oil
4	eggs, beaten
3	cups grated raw carrots

Preheat oven to 325 degrees.

Mix all ingredients together except carrots. Add carrots last and mix well. (Batter will be thin.) Pour cake mixture into either a greased and floured 9 by 13-inch flat pan or into 2 greased and floured 8-inch round cake pans. Bake 45 to 50 minutes in flat pan; 35 to 40 minutes in round pans. Let cool completely before frosting.

Frosting:

8	ounces cream cheese, softened
2	teaspoons vanilla
5	tablespoons margarine, softened
1	1-pound box confectioners' sugar

Combine all ingredients and beat until smooth. Spread over top and sides of cake and between layers, if using rounds.

Makes 8 to 10 servings.

MEL TILLIS' PUMPKIN CHEESECAKE

Mel's father ran a bakery in Florida and when Mel joined the Air Force he says, "I became a baker, too." A statement to which this heavenly dessert will attest.

Nut Crust:
2   cups ground pecans
2   tablespoons brown sugar
1   egg white, beaten until frothy
1   teaspoon powdered ginger
1   teaspoon finely grated lemon rind

Mix all ingredients together just until mixture is bound together. Press into the bottom and up the sides of a 10-inch springform pan.

Cake Batter:
2½   pounds cream cheese, softened
1   cup granulated sugar
4   large eggs, lightly beaten
3   egg yolks, lightly beaten
3   tablespoons all-purpose flour
2   teaspoons ground cinnamon
1   teaspoon ground cloves
1   teaspoon ground ginger
2   teaspoons finely grated lemon rind
1   cup heavy cream
1   tablespoon vanilla
1   16-ounce can pumpkin puree
    Coarsely grated lemon rind for garnish

Preheat oven to 425 degrees.

Beat together cream cheese, sugar, eggs, and egg yolks. Add flour, cinnamon, cloves, ginger and lemon rind. Beat in cream and vanilla. Add pumpkin and beat until thoroughly mixed.

Pour into prepared nut crust and bake 15 minutes at 425 degrees. Reduce heat to 275 degrees and bake an hour longer. Turn off heat and allow cake to cool overnight or for 8 hours in the oven. Refrigerate for several hours or overnight. Garnish with grated lemon rind before serving.

Makes 16 servings.

KITTY WELLS' ORANGE COCONUT CAKE

The icing on Kitty's cake will have your friends asking for the recipe.

½	cup shortening
1	cup sugar
1	teaspoon vanilla
½	teaspoon orange extract
2	eggs
2	cups sifted cake flour
1	teaspoon baking powder
¾	teaspoon soda
¼	teaspoon salt
1	cup buttermilk

Preheat oven to 350 degrees.

Stir shortening to soften. Gradually add sugar and cream until light and fluffy. Add extracts. Add eggs, one at a time, beating well after each. Sift together dry ingredients. Add to creamed mixture alternately with buttermilk, beginning and ending with flour. Beat after each addition. Bake in 2 8-inch square pans for 30 minutes. Cool.

Icing:

1	cup water
2	cups sugar
2	egg whites
3	teaspoons grated orange peel
½	cup sugar
1	whole coconut, grated, or 1 package of grated coconut
	Juice of 3 oranges

Bring sugar and water to a boil. Cook to soft boil stage. Gradually add hot syrup to egg whites, beating constantly. Beat until frosting is of spreading consistency. After cake has cooled, spread on icing, then cover with the grated orange peel mixed with ½ cup sugar, orange juice and coconut.

Makes 12 servings.

BARBARA MANDRELL'S KNOBBY APPLE CAKE

Barbara suggests, "while still warm, top this cake with whipped cream or vanilla ice cream and serve."

2   tablespoons butter, softened
1   cup sugar
1   egg, beaten
1   cup all-purpose flour
½   teaspoon cinnamon
½   teaspoon nutmeg
½   teaspoon salt
1   teaspoon baking soda
3   cups peeled, cored and chopped apples
½   cup chopped pecans
1   teaspoon vanilla
    Whipped cream or ice cream (optional)

Preheat oven to 350 degrees.

Cream butter and sugar; add egg and mix well. In a separate bowl mix together dry ingredients and add to the creamed mixture. Mix well. Stir in apples, nuts and vanilla. Pour into a greased 8 by 10-inch baking pan. Bake for 45 minutes.

Makes 12 servings.

BILL ANDERSON'S ORANGE CAKE

The apricot nectar gives a fruity taste to a usual yellow cake.

1   18¼-ounce box yellow cake mix
1   tablespoon lemon extract
¾   cup vegetable oil
1   cup apricot nectar juice
4   eggs, separated

Preheat oven to 325 degrees.

Mix cake mix, lemon extract, oil, nectar and egg yolks until well blended. In a separate bowl, beat egg whites until stiff. Fold into batter and pour into a greased 9-inch tube pan. Bake for 45 minutes to an hour. Use a cake tester or toothpick to test for doneness.

Glaze:
1½   cups confectioners' sugar
     Juice of 2 lemons

Blend the sugar and lemon juice and pour over cake while still hot.

Makes 8 to 10 servings.

BARBARA MANDRELL'S PEACH SHORTCAKE

When buying peaches, pick fruit that has an underlying cream or yellow tone. You may store ripe peaches in the fridge, unwashed, for 1 to 2 weeks.

8-10 fresh peaches
     Sugar to taste
1   3½-ounce package vanilla instant pudding
1   pint whipping cream
1   teaspoon vanilla
1   1-pound Sara Lee (or homemade) pound cake

Peel and slice peaches and add sugar to taste. Let stand to make juices.

Prepare instant pudding according to package directions, using peach juices as part of liquid.

Whip cream until stiff peaks appear. Add vanilla and sugar to taste.

Serve in layers beginning with a slice of pound cake, then pudding, peaches and whipped cream. Garnish with a fresh peach slice on top.

Makes 8 to 10 servings.

REBA McENTIRE'S STRAWBERRY COBBLER

Reba's cobbler is a favorite recipe donated by Norma Jones, mother of Reba's bus driver.

2   10-ounce bags frozen strawberries
¾   cup water
2½   cups sugar
1½   cups flour
1   tablespoon baking powder
1   cup milk
½   cup butter or margarine, melted

Preheat oven to 300 degrees.

Thaw strawberries and mix with ¾ cup water. Mash strawberries and water together with 1 cup sugar; set aside.

Mix flour with remaining 1½ cups sugar, baking powder and milk. Pour melted butter in 9 by 13-inch glass baking dish. Pour in flour mixture. Pour strawberry mixture on top of flour mixture. Bake 40 to 50 minutes.

Editors Note: You may substitute other fruits for a variety of delicious cobblers.

Makes 8 servings.

THE STATLER BROTHERS' MERINGUE-TOPPED STRAWBERRY SHORTCAKE

Strawberry shortcake is a classic, just like the Statlers!

1	quart fresh strawberries, washed and hulled
¾	cup granulated sugar
2⅓	cups Bisquick baking mix
3	tablespoons granulated sugar
3	tablespoons margarine or butter, melted
½	cup milk
2	egg whites
¼	cup confectioners' sugar
1	tablespoon granulated sugar

Slice strawberries and place in bowl; sprinkle with ½ cup granulated sugar and let stand 1 hour.

Preheat oven to 375 degrees.

Mix Bisquick, 3 tablespoons granulated sugar, margarine and milk until soft dough forms. Gently smooth into a ball on cloth-covered board dusted with Bisquick. Knead 8 to 10 times. Pat into ungreased 9-inch round pan.

In mixing bowl, beat egg whites until foamy. Beat in confectioners' sugar and ¼ cup granulated sugar, 1 tablespoon at a time; continue beating until egg whites are stiff and glossy. Spread meringue on dough; sprinkle with 1 tablespoon granulated sugar.

Bake until delicate brown, 25 or 30 minutes. Remove and cool 10 minutes. Run knife around edge of pan to loosen; turn onto cloth-covered board. Invert on wire rack; cool completely. Serve with strawberries spooned on top.

Makes 8 servings.

MINNIE PEARL'S CHESS PIE

Minnie states uncategorically that she chose all the recipes she's included in this cookbook, "because they're deliciously fattening!"

1	8-inch unbaked pie shell
½	cup butter or margarine
1½	cups sugar
3	eggs, beaten
1	tablespoon cider vinegar
1	tablespoon vanilla
½	teaspoon salt

Prepare pie shell.

Preheat oven to 300 degrees.

Combine the butter and sugar in saucepan over medium heat. Cook, stirring constantly, until very smooth. Remove pan from the heat. Add eggs and mix thoroughly. Stir in vinegar, vanilla and salt; beat well with a wire whisk. Pour into pie shell and bake for 50 minutes.

Makes 6 to 8 servings.

RICKY SKAGGS' CHESS PIE

A popular Southern dessert from an artist who labels himself "as country as cornbread."

1	9-inch unbaked pie shell
2	eggs, beaten
1	cup white sugar
½	cup brown sugar
½	cup melted butter
1	tablespoon vanilla
1	tablespoon cornmeal
1	tablespoon all-purpose flour
¼	cup milk
½	teaspoon vinegar

Prepare your favorite pie pastry.

Preheat oven to 325 degrees.

Mix together all ingredients well; pour into pie shell. Bake for 40 to 45 minutes, or until pie tests done.

Makes 6 to 8 servings.

THE WHITES' PECAN PIE

This rich pie is from the kitchen of the Whites' favorite cook — Sharon and Cheryl's mother Patty!

1   9-inch unbaked pie shell
½   cup butter, softened
½   cup sugar
¾   cup white corn syrup
2   tablespoons strained honey
3   eggs, slightly beaten
1   teaspoon vanilla
2   cups chopped pecans

Prepare pie shell.

Preheat oven to 350 degrees.

In a large bowl cream butter until soft. Add sugar gradually, continuing to cream until light and fluffy. Slowly stir in syrup, honey, eggs, vanilla and 1 cup pecans. Pour into pie shell and place remaining pecans evenly on top.

Bake for 50 to 55 minutes, or until done.

Makes 6 to 8 servings.

BRENDA LEE'S DEEP DISH GEORGIA PEACH PIE

A peach of a recipe specialty from a peach of a singer who taught herself to cook and likes what she's learned: "It gives me great satisfaction when it's edible!"

6   cups fresh peaches, peeled and sliced
1   cup sugar
3   tablespoons cornstarch
1   tablespoon lemon juice (optional)
     Pastry for one-crust pie

Preheat oven to 400 degrees.

Gently mix ingredients (except pastry!) together. Pour mixture into 9-inch square pan.

Roll out pastry and shape into a square to fit pan. Make small slits in center of pastry to let steam escape during baking. Lay crust over filling. Bake 50 to 60 minutes or until crust is browned.

Makes 8 servings.

BARBARA MANDRELL'S STRAWBERRY PIE

Barbara's recipe is as delicious tasting as it is delicious looking. It is particularly nice for a summertime cookout.

1   9-inch baked pie shell
½   cup sifted confectioners' sugar
1   quart fresh strawberries, washed and hulled
1   cup water
1½   tablespoons cornstarch
½-¾ cup granulated sugar (depending on how
          sweet you want the berries)
1   cup heavy cream, whipped

Prepare baked pie shell.

Add confectioners' sugar to 3 cups whole fresh strawberries. Let stand for one hour. Crush remaining cup of berries and cook in water about 2 minutes. Drain through sieve or strainer. Mix cornstarch and granulated sugar and stir into berries. Cook gently until clear, stirring constantly.

Fill pie shell with whole berries and pour the strawberry sauce over them. Chill. Top with whipped cream.

Makes 6 to 8 servings.

THE OAK RIDGE BOYS' LEMONADE PIE

A melt-in-your-mouth summer treat given to The Oak Ridge Boys by Judy Chaplain.

Crust:
½   cup butter, softened
2   tablespoons sugar
2¼- 2½ cups all-purpose flour

Preheat oven to 375 degrees.

Soften butter with sugar. Add flour and mix well. Set aside ¼ of the mixture for topping. Press remainder in a 9-inch pie pan evenly along sides and bottom. Bake 12 to 15 minutes. Cool. Crumble topping mixture and place in small pan and bake at the same time as crust for 10 to 12 minutes.

Filling:
1   egg white
       Yellow food coloring
½   cup sugar
½   of a 6-ounce can frozen lemonade, partly thawed
1   cup whipping cream

Beat egg white until it forms soft peaks. Add food coloring. Beat in sugar gradually until stiff. Fold in lemonade. Beat whipping cream until thick. Fold into lemonade mixture and pour into pie shell. Spread baked crumbs evenly on top. Freeze until firm. Serve.

Makes 6 to 8 servings.

BOBBY BARE'S CHOCOLATE CREAM PIE

Bobby's old-fashioned chocolate cream pie will remind you of the one your grandmother probably served.

Pie Shell:

1	cup all-purpose flour
1/2	teaspoon salt
2	tablespoons sugar
6	tablespoons vegetable shortening
2	tablespoons water (more or less)

Preheat oven to 450 degrees.

To prepare pie shell, mix all dry ingredients together. Cut in the shortening. Sprinkle in water. Mix well and turn out on floured board. Roll out to 2 inches larger than the pie plate. Place in pie plate. Seal by pressing side edges with fingers. Fill pie shell with crust weights and bake for 8 minutes or until golden brown. Cool. Remove weights and fill with chocolate cream filling.

Chocolate Cream Filling:

4	egg yolks
1	cup sugar
3 1/2	tablespoons cocoa
1 1/2	cups evaporated milk
1 1/2	cups water
4	tablespoons cornstarch

Beat together egg yolks and sugar. Add cocoa, milk and 1/2 cup water. Place in pan and bring to a boil, stirring so it will not stick to pan. Mix together remaining cup of water and cornstarch, making sure there are no lumps, and add this to the filling.

Stir mixture over heat until thickened. Remove from heat and cool, stirring occasionally to avoid crust forming on top. Pour into pie shell and cool until chocolate is set.

Makes 6 to 8 servings.

Editors Note: If weights for the crust are not available, prick the bottom of the crust with a fork in several places before baking to keep it from puffing.

THE OAK RIDGE BOYS' PUMPKIN PIE

A favorite of Joe Bonsall and we are sure it will be a favorite of yours, too.

1	9-inch unbaked pie shell
2	eggs, slightly beaten
1½	cups solid pack canned pumpkin
¾	cup sugar
½	teaspoon salt
1	teaspoon cinnamon
½	teaspoon ginger
¼	teaspoon cloves
1⅔	cups evaporated milk

Prepare pie shell.

Preheat oven to 425 degrees.

Mix ingredients in order given. Pour into pie shell. Bake at 425 degrees for 15 minutes, then reduce to 350 degrees and bake for 45 to 50 minutes or until knife inserted comes out clean.

Makes 6 to 8 servings.

LEE GREENWOOD'S PUMPKIN PIE

Many of the country music artists in this cookbook named Thanksgiving and Christmas as the best meals of the year. And pumpkin pie is a favorite on those special days!

1	9-inch uncooked pastry shell
1	16-ounce can pumpkin (about 2 cups)
1	14-ounce can sweetened condensed milk
2	eggs, beaten
1	teaspoon ground cinnamon
½	teaspoon ground ginger
½	teaspoon ground nutmeg
½	teaspoon salt
	Whipped cream and nuts (optional)

Prepare pastry shell.

Preheat oven to 425 degrees.

In a large bowl, combine all ingredients (except whipped cream and nuts); mix well and turn into the pastry shell. Bake for 15 minutes; reduce oven temperature to 350 degrees and continue baking 35 to 40 minutes or until knife inserted 1 inch from edge comes out clean. Cool before slicing.

Garnish with whipped cream and nuts if desired. Refrigerate leftovers, if any.

Makes 8 servings.

JERRY REED'S SWEET POTATO PIE

Jerry loves what he calls "good old Southern cooking"... meat loaf, dried beans, fried okra and corn, mashed potatoes, sliced onions, iced tea and, of course, sweet potato pie.

4   large sweet potatoes
½   cup margarine, softened
1   cup sugar
1   tablespoon nutmeg
1   9-inch baked pie shell

Peel potatoes and boil until soft. Drain. Add other ingredients and mix thoroughly. Put into baked pie crust. Serve.

Makes 1 9-inch pie.

Editors Note: Whipped cream makes a nice topping on this pie.

HELEN CORNELIUS' SWEET SOUTHERN PASTRY

This is a wonderfully rich pie crust. Try it with the recipes in this book that call for your favorite pie crust.

1½   cups all-purpose flour
2   tablespoons sugar
1   teaspoon baking powder
½   teaspoon salt
1   egg yolk, beaten
4   tablespoons ice water
½   cup vegetable shortening

Sift dry ingredients in a bowl. Mix egg yolk with ice water. Blend the shortening in with dry ingredients and make into dough with egg yolk, ice water mixture. Roll out to about ⅛-inch thick and line a 9-inch pie pan.

Makes 1 pie crust.

Editors Note: If your recipe calls for a baked pie crust, bake in a preheated oven at 450 degrees for 12 to 15 minutes or until lightly browned. (So crust does not buckle while baking, place pie weights on crust, or white rice on waxed paper will do the same.) Note directions on individual recipe if baking a filled pie.

DOLLY PARTON'S APPLE STACK PIE

Dolly and her band and road crew enjoy roadside picnics with homemade foods, rather than stopping at restaurants. We'd bet that this pie goes along to some of those picnics!

6	cups self-rising flour
½	teaspoon baking soda
1	cup butter
4	eggs, beaten
½	cup molasses
1	cup sugar
1	teaspoon vanilla
1	teaspoon cinnamon
⅔	cup milk

Sift together flour and soda; add butter and mix well. Beat together eggs, molasses, sugar, vanilla, cinnamon and milk. Add flour mixture and mix until it looks like bread dough. Turn onto a floured board or cloth and knead for a few seconds. Divide the dough into six equal layers, and roll out into thin layers like pie crust. Grease flour six round cake or pie pans. Put one layer into each pan and pat flat. Bake for 10 to 15 minutes at 300 degrees. Remove from pans and cool.

Filling:

1	pound apples-peeled, cored and sliced
½	cup water
½	cup sugar
¼	teaspoon cinnamon
⅛	teaspoon allspice filling

Cook apples slowly in water until soft. Strain. To each cup of pulp add ½ cup sugar and cinnamon and allspice. Cook over low heat until sugar is dissolved, and until mixture is thick. Place filling between layers, and stack one layer on top of the other. This recipe will make two 3-layer cakes or one 6-layer cake. This cake is best after it sits for 2 or 3 days

Makes 10 to 12 servings.

THE STATLER BROTHERS' EASY APPLE CRUMB PIE

Apple varieties especially good for pies are Cortland, Granny Smith, Jonathan, McIntosh and Rome Beauty.

5	cooking apples, cored, peeled and sliced
	Cinnamon
1	cup sugar
1	cup all-purpose flour
½	cup butter, softened

Preheat oven to 375 degrees.

Slightly grease 9-inch square casserole dish. Place apples to cover bottom of dish. Sprinkle apples with cinnamon. In bowl, mix sugar and flour. Add butter and cream with a fork to make crumbs. Sprinkle mixture over apples. Bake for 30 minutes until golden brown.

Makes 6 to 8 servings.

Editors Note: Add additional apples if 5 are not enough to cover bottom of baking dish.

T.G. SHEPPARD'S PRALINE CRACKERS

These are easy to make and especially fun if you have little ones in the kitchen who want to "help."

20-24 whole graham crackers
1   cup butter
1   cup light brown sugar
1   cup chopped pecans

Preheat oven to 350 degrees.

Line cookie sheet with the graham crackers. In saucepan, melt butter, then add the sugar and pecans. Boil for 2 minutes. Be sure to time this, or the mixture will harden. Spoon mixture evenly over crackers and bake for 10 minutes. Remove from cookie sheet and cool on wire rack.

Makes 20 to 24 Pralines.

EARL THOMAS CONLEY'S CHOCOLATE FUDGE

Terrific for chocolate lovers!

3   cups sugar
      Pinch salt
2/3   cup cocoa
1 1/2 cups milk
1/4   cup butter
1   teaspoon vanilla
1/2   cup chopped nuts (optional)

In saucepan, mix sugar, salt and cocoa. Add milk gradually. Cook on medium heat, stirring constantly. Cook until soft ball stage. Test by dropping small amount of mixture in cold water. If it forms soft ball, remove from heat.

Add butter and vanilla, mix well. Set pan in cold water; stir until shine is almost gone. Add nuts if desired. Pour into 8-inch square buttered dish and let cool.

Make 16 small squares.

THE OAK RIDGE BOYS' GERMAN CHOCOLATE CARAMEL SQUARES

Chewy and richly delicious!

1   14-ounce package light caramels
2/3   cup evaporated milk
1   18¼-ounce box German chocolate cake mix
¾   cup butter, softened
1   cup chopped nuts
1   cup semi-sweet chocolate chips

Preheat oven to 350 degrees.

In top of double boiler, melt caramels and ⅓ cup milk over low heat, stirring constantly. Remove from heat but leave in double boiler over hot water so as not to harden.

Blend cake mix, butter and ⅓ cup milk. Pour cake mixture into greased 13 by 9-inch baking dish. Bake for 6 minutes. Sprinkle nuts and chocolate chips on top. Pour caramel mix over chips and nuts, then add the rest of cake mix. Bake another 20 minutes. Cool and cut into squares.

Makes 12 squares.

B. J. THOMAS' FUDGE BROWNIES

Brownies are also yummy crumbled up on vanilla or chocolate ice cream.

½   cup butter or margarine
2   1-ounce squares unsweetened chocolate
1   cup granulated sugar
2   eggs
1   teaspoon vanilla
¾   cup sifted all-purpose flour

Preheat oven to 350 degrees.

In medium saucepan, melt butter and chocolate. Remove from heat; stir in sugar. Blend in eggs one at a time. Add vanilla. Stir in the flour; mix well.

Spread batter in 8-inch square greased baking dish. Bake for 30 minutes. Cool. Cut into squares.

Makes 16 brownies.

THE STATLER BROTHERS' CHOCOLATE-PEANUT BUTTER BALLS

Guests and family alike will be coming back for more of these.

1	cup graham cracker crumbs
1	pound box confectioners' sugar
1	cup shredded coconut
½	cup crunchy peanut butter
1	cup melted butter
1	16-ounce bag chocolate chips
½	block paraffin

Mix together all ingredients except chocolate chips and paraffin. Form into 1-inch round balls and place on cookie sheet covered with waxed paper. Stick toothpick into each. Place in refrigerator to cool.

Melt chocolate chips with paraffin. Dip each ball and drop on waxed paper. Cool and serve.

Makes about 3 dozen.

THE OAK RIDGE BOYS' PEANUT BUTTER BARS

Peanut butter rich! These bars are great served as dessert with a fresh fruit cup.

¾	cup butter
¾	cup sugar
¾	cup brown sugar
1½	cups all-purpose flour
¾	teaspoon baking soda
½	teaspoon salt
½	cup peanut butter
1	teaspoon vanilla
1½	cups oatmeal
1	6-ounce package chocolate chips

Preheat oven to 350 degrees. Cream until smooth butter, sugar and brown sugar.

Mix together flour, soda and salt. Blend into butter and sugar and add peanut butter, vanilla and oatmeal.

Spread mixture in buttered cookie sheet with ½-inch sides and bake for 20 to 25 minutes. Sprinkle immediately after removing from oven with chocolate chips. Let chocolate stand for 5 minutes, then spread around evenly.

Makes about 1½ to 2 dozen.

BOBBY BARE'S PEANUT BRITTLE

*Your youngsters will love this —
and so will the adults.*

2 cups sugar
1/16 teaspoon baking soda
1/8 teaspoon salt
1 cup chopped unsalted peanuts

Melt sugar in a frying pan over low heat until light brown. Stir carefully and do not burn. Add soda and salt and stir well. Spread peanuts in a single layer in an 8 by 8-inch buttered pan. Pour sugar mixture gradually over peanuts. Do not stir. Allow to cool as a thin sheet of candy. Remove from pan and break into pieces.

Makes 1/2 pound.

Editors Note: When storing peanut brittle, make sure you do so in an airtight container.

DEBORAH ALLEN'S CHOCOLATE OATMEAL COOKIES

*You may use a combination of
chocolate chips and pecans in
these cookies. Use one-half the
amount of each.*

1 egg
1/4 cup water
1 1/2 cups sugar
1 cup margarine or butter, softened
1 teaspoon vanilla
1 1/4 cups all-purpose flour
1/3 cup cocoa
1/2 teaspoon salt
1/2 teaspoon baking soda
3 cups quick-cooking oats
1 6-ounce package semisweet chocolate chips or
  1 cup chopped pecans

Preheat oven to 350 degrees.

Beat egg and water together; add sugar, margarine and vanilla. Mix well.

Combine flour, cocoa, salt, baking soda and oats. Add to egg mixture. Blend thoroughly. Add chocolate chips or pecans. Mix well.

Drop dough by rounded teaspoonful, placing 2 inches apart on ungreased cookie sheet. Bake at 350 degrees for 10 minutes or until golden. Immediately remove from cookie sheet to wire rack.

Makes about 5 1/2 dozen cookies.

HELEN CORNELIUS' OATMEAL COOKIES

As a child, Helen's contribution to the dining table was cookies. She also says, "I always took them to our youth meetings at church and I really took pride in making them."

1	cup raisins
6	tablespoons raisin juice from cooked raisins
1	teaspoon baking soda
2	eggs
¾	cup sugar
¾	cup brown sugar
1	cup shortening
1	teaspoon vanilla
2	cups all-purpose flour
1	teaspoon baking powder
½	teaspoon salt
1	teaspoon cinnamon
2	cups oatmeal
¾	cup chopped nuts

In a saucepan, simmer raisins with water to cover for about 30 minutes over low heat. Drain and reserve juice.

Preheat oven to 375 degrees.

Dissolve baking soda in raisin juice. In a bowl, beat eggs with fork until blended. Cream in sugar, shortening and vanilla. Add cooked raisins and raisin juice.

Sift together flour, baking powder, salt and cinnamon. Add to egg and raisin mixture. Stir in oatmeal. Add nuts and stir until well blended. Drop by teaspoons onto greased cookie sheet. Bake in 375-degree oven about 8 to 10 minutes or until golden brown. Remove to wire rack to cool.

Makes about 5 dozen 2½-inch cookies.

Editors Note: Either pecans or walnuts work for this recipe. You may wish to divide the batter and use a different nut in each half.

EMMYLOU HARRIS' SHERRIED FRUIT

Excellent to round off a meal of Emmylou's Chicken Eleganté, page 131.

1   8-ounce can each:
    pineapple chunks
    peach halves
    pears
    apricots
1   8-ounce jar spiced apple rings

Drain fruit and put in large bowl. In top of a double boiler, combine:

2   tablespoons all-purpose flour
½   cup brown sugar
½   cup butter
1   cup sherry

Cook over boiling water until bubbly. Pour mixture over fruit. Keep refrigerated until needed. To serve, put fruit in casserole and heat at 350 degrees until bubbly.

Makes 12 servings.

Editors Note: Cut up fresh fruit may be substituted. Use 1 cup of each kind of fruit.

T. G. SHEPPARD'S BAKED APRICOTS

Delicious alone or served with vanilla ice cream.

2   16-ounce cans peeled apricot halves
½   cup light brown sugar
1   12-ounce box Ritz crackers, crumbled
4   tablespoons butter

Preheat oven to 300 degrees.

In a 9 by 9-inch greased baking dish, place a layer of apricots and cover lightly with brown sugar. Add a layer of crumbled Ritz crackers, then dot thickly with lumps of butter. Repeat this to the top of the dish and bake for 1 hour.

Makes 8 servings.

DOLLY PARTON'S BANANA PUDDING

This special dessert is Dolly's treat at Aunt Granny's Restaurant in "Dollywood."

2   12-ounce boxes vanilla wafers ('Nilla* wafers)
3   pounds bananas, sliced
1½ cups sugar
½   cup all-purpose flour
6   egg yolks
3   whole eggs
½   cup butter
    Dash salt
6   cups milk
2   teaspoons vanilla

Layer sliced bananas and vanilla wafers in large baking pan. Mix together sugar, flour, eggs, butter and salt in heavy-bottomed saucepan. Add the milk, a little at a time. Cook slowly until the mixture thickens. Let it cool for a few minutes, then add the vanilla. Pour over bananas and vanilla wafers.

Meringue topping:
6   egg whites
1   teaspoon lemon juice
1   teaspoon sugar
1   teaspoon vanilla

Beat the 6 egg whites with lemon juice, sugar and vanilla until stiff. Spoon this mixture over the top of the pudding and brown at 350 degrees for 10 to 12 minutes or until golden on top.

Makes 10 to 12 servings.

CONWAY TWITTY'S CRUNCHY BAKED BANANAS

Conway loves food using bananas. Try this favorite Twitty banana recipe.

2   large or 3 small bananas
½   cup miniature marshmallows
2   tablespoons brown sugar
1   cup cornflakes, crumbled
1   tablespoon butter, melted

Preheat oven to 375 degrees.

Cut bananas in half lengthwise. Place them, sliced edges up, in a buttered baking dish. Mix together the marshmallows and brown sugar; sprinkle evenly over the bananas. Combine cornflakes and butter and sprinkle on top. Bake for 12 minutes.

Makes 4 to 6 servings.

TAMMY WYNETTE'S BANANA PUDDING

"Banana Pudding," says Tammy, "is one of my favorite foods I learned to make as a child."

1	12-ounce box Vanilla wafers
1	cup self-rising flour
2½	cups sugar
6	eggs, separated
6	cups milk
1	teaspoon vanilla
6	bananas, sliced

Crumble enough vanilla wafers to cover bottom of 9 by 13-inch glass baking dish to 1-inch thickness. Set aside.

Preheat oven to 350 degrees.

Combine flour and 2 cups sugar in top of a double boiler and mix thoroughly. Add egg yolks and mix well. Gradually add milk to the mixture and blend until smooth. Add vanilla and cook over simmering water at medium temperature until thickened, stirring continuously. Allow to cool to room temperature. Pour mixture over wafers and cover evenly with sliced bananas.

Beat egg whites in mixing bowl, gradually adding remaining ½ cup sugar. Beat until stiff. Spread meringue over bananas and brown for 8 to 10 minutes until golden brown.

Makes 8 servings.

THE STATLER BROTHERS' CUSTARD

To keep a crust from forming on your custard, cover the top with plastic wrap immediately after pouring into a casserole or small dishes.

1	gallon milk
12	eggs
3	cups sugar
2	tablespoons vanilla

In a large pot, slowly heat milk over medium heat stirring constantly. Remove from heat. In a large bowl, beat eggs, sugar and vanilla. Stir into milk and bring to a boil, continuing to stir. Cook until the custard coats a spoon.

Pour custard into casseroles or individual dishes. Chill until firm and serve.

Makes 24 to 30 servings.

Editors Note: This recipe divides well for smaller amounts. For instance: dividing by 4 — 1 quart milk, 3 eggs, ¾ cup sugar and ½ teaspoon vanilla. Makes 6 servings.

THE OAK RIDGE BOYS' HOMEMADE ICE CREAM

This ice cream recipe is for a 1 gallon ice cream freezer. It is a special treat served for Duane Allen by his mom.

5   *medium eggs*
2⅓ *cups sugar*
2   *14-ounce cans Carnation evaporated milk*
1½ *teaspoons vanilla*
    Pinch salt
    Milk
    Fruits and nuts (optional)

Beat eggs well with mixer until very light in color. Add sugar, milk, vanilla and salt. Beat well for 2 more minutes. Pour into 4-quart cooler and finish filling up with whole milk within 1 inch of top. Stir. Freeze 20 to 25 minutes. You may add fruits and ground nuts.

Makes 8 to 10 servings.

DEBORAH ALLEN'S HOT RUM SAUCE

Deborah suggests serving her hot rum sauce over ice cream or vanilla pudding.

1   *cup brown sugar, packed*
1   *teaspoon all-purpose flour*
½ *cup butter*
½ *cup boiling water*
⅓-½ *cup rum*

In a saucepan, place brown sugar, flour and butter. Blend thoroughly and add boiling water. Cook over low heat, stirring, until mixture thickens and is clear. Remove from heat and stir in rum. Start with ⅓ cup first and add more to taste.

Makes 8 servings.

LEE GREENWOOD'S FOUR-LAYER DESSERT

Lee enjoys cooking and especially likes "down home fare." If you're a pudding lover, this dessert's for you — from Lee.

1 cup all-purpose flour
1 cup finely chopped nuts
½ cup margarine, melted
1 8-ounce package cream cheese, softened
1 cup sifted confectioners' sugar
1 cup frozen non-dairy whipped topping, thawed
1 4⅛ ounce package chocolate instant pudding mix
1 3¾ ounce package vanilla instant pudding mix
   Whipped topping and nuts (optional)

Preheat oven to 350 degrees.

Combine flour, nuts and margarine; mix well. Press onto bottom of 11¾ by x 7½-inch baking dish. Bake for 15 minutes. Cool.

Combine cream cheese and sugar, mixing until well-blended. Fold in whipped topping; spread over crust. Chill for 1 hour.

Prepare chocolate pudding as directed on package and spread over cream cheese mixture. Chill 1 hour more.

Prepare vanilla pudding as directed on package and spread over chocolate pudding. Chill 1 hour or more.

Cut into squares. Garnish with additional whipped topping and nuts, if desired.

Makes 8 servings.

TANYA TUCKER'S
FIVE-MINUTE ORANGE HASH DESSERT

A "cool-light" summer dessert that only takes five minutes to prepare. Tanya and friend "T" Martin highly recommend it.

1   3-ounce box orange Jell-O
1   8-ounce package of cream cheese, softened
1   8-ounce container Cool Whip whipped topping
1   3-ounce can mandarin oranges, drained
1   cup chopped pecans

Place dry jello, cream cheese and Cool Whip in a bowl and beat well; add mandarin oranges and mix. Add pecans and stir. Should you like the consistency to be a little thinner, add juice of mandarin oranges. Chill in 8 by 8-inch pan until firm, about 3 hours. Cut into squares and serve.

Makes 6 to 8 servings.

RONNIE MILSAP'S MOONSHINE

The non-alcoholic kind!

10   apples, peeled, cored and quartered
2   bunches of carrots, tops removed and chopped
1   stalk celery, chopped

Blend all together for a quick and healthy pick-me-up!

Editors Note: A juice extractor is needed to blend this properly. If you do not own one process vegetables in a blender or food processor and add apple or pineapple juice to make a smooth consistency.

Makes a lot!

TOM T. HALL'S WATERMELON WINE

With songs like "Old Dogs, Children and Watermelon Wine" and recipes like this, it's clear that Tom T. has a keen, cock-eyed appreciation for the unusual.

1   large watermelon
1   quart "moonshine" (vodka may be substituted)

Plug watermelon and mash insides! To accomplish this, cut a hole in the top of the watermelon just large enough to fit the neck of the "moonshine" or vodka bottle. Remove the bottle's cap and up-end the bottle in the hole, allowing the liquid to seep slowly into the fruit.

Remove the bottle. Chill the watermelon thoroughly. Slice and serve.

Number of servings depends on size of watermelon and size of slices.

KENNY ROGERS' HOT MULLED PUNCH

Kenny's punch is great on cold, brisk days. And it is a special treat at holiday time.

1   quart Kraft pure 100% unsweetened pasteurized orange juice
3   cups apple cider
1/4   cup sugar
1/4   cup packed brown sugar
1/4   teaspoon allspice
1/8   teaspoon ground cloves
      Soft Parkay margarine
      Cinnamon sticks

Combine orange juice, cider, sugars and spices in 2-quart saucepan. Bring to boil and simmer 5 minutes.

For each serving, pour pouch into mugs; top with dollop of margarine. Stir and serve with cinnamon stick.

Makes 1½ quarts.

B.J. Thomas

A native of Hugo, Oklahoma, reared in Houston, Texas, B.J. (short for "Billy Joe") Thomas is country born and bred. But his favorite food is not from *this* country. "I enjoy any kind of Italian food, especially pasta," he admits. His favorite is fettucini with white cream sauce. And his favorite cook is Mario Ferrari, owner of Mario's, a Nashville restaurant specializing in northern Italian cuisine.

Although B.J. is no four-star chef, he knows his way around the kitchen pretty well and enjoys cooking for himself from time to time. "I like to cook because I like to prepare my food just the way I want it," he says. He also enjoys cooking for the rest of the family as an excuse for getting together. "I enjoy cooking meals for my family: my wife, Gloria; and my daughters Paige, Nora and Erin. Gloria and I like getting into the kitchen and preparing new and interesting meals for the kids. Our whole family enjoys dining together when we can." The holidays are a particularly good time for getting together. "My favorite holiday meal is the traditional turkey and dressing with all the trimmings (hot homemade rolls, cranberry sauce, pecan pie). The traditional meal always puts me in the holiday spirit."

B.J.'s biggest hit, "Raindrops Keep Fallin' On My Head," went to #1 on the pop charts, and he has since had big crossover hits with "Hooked on a Feeling," "Hey Won't You Play (Another Somebody Done Somebody Wrong Song)" and "Two Car Garage." One of his biggest thrills came in August, 1981 when he became the Opry's sixtieth member. "My dad was my first motivation to be a singer," he says, "but the Grand Ole Opry was the first inspiration for my music. The Opry has such an influence on my early life, dating back to seeing Hank Williams in person when I was in the third grade." Later, B.J.'s first million-selling song was a Hank Williams tune, "I'm So Lonesome I Could Cry."

Being in demand on the road means that B.J. can't get home-cooked meals and good pasta as often as he'd like. "My band and I travel primarily by tour bus," he says, "so we eat a lot of fast food along the way." Even when he's away from home, though, he still gets a memorable meal occasionally. "In December, 1982," he recalls, "I dined with Willie Nelson, golfer Lee Trevino, Darrell Royal, former head coach of the University of Texas football team, and Darrell's wife, Edith. We dined at the Royals' lakehouse in Austin. Edith prepared a delicious Texas-style stew and cornbread."

Even B.J. would admit that that kind of country cooking and hospitality beats Italian food any day — with the exception of maybe his fettucini Alfredo or veal scallopini. Judge for yourself.

Mel Tillis is always right at home on the range — be it wood or electric. "I love to cook," he says. "My father was a baker and ran a small, independent bakery in Pahokee, Florida. He made the best jelly rolls and honey buns in South Florida. When I went into the Air Force, I became a baker, too. I still enjoy getting in the kitchen and whipping things up." And he's still his own favorite cook despite his first experience with a meat smoker when Mel "ruined about six-hundred dollars worth of beef."

Mel's folks didn't have much money when he was growing up. So, as soon as he was able, he picked strawberries for three cents a quart to help make ends meet. "We were poor," he says, "but there was always plenty of fresh fruits and vegetables." Today, getting a nutritious meal is still difficult for Mel, but for different reasons: with a full schedule of TV, movie and concert appearances, he is in a hurry almost year round. "I try to eat as sensibly as possible while on the road," he says. "That includes a good breakfast with bacon, eggs, biscuits and grapefruit. Being a native Floridian, naturally I love all types of citrus and fresh vegetables." He's also a big fan of Japanese food.

His favorite meal, though, is strictly country: pork chops, turnip greens, potato salad, cornbread, sliced tomatoes, onions and lots of milk. It's the sort of meal that Mel likes to linger over at home with wife Judy; daughters Pamela, Connie, Cindy, and Carrie; and son Mel Jr. "Nowadays I cherish every meal with my family," he says, "because I'm gone most of the time and I don't get to eat with them very often."

Mel got to be as busy as he is today mostly because of his talent, but also because he made the most of a shortcoming. He started out in Nashville as a songwriter, penning such hits as "Detroit City" for Bobby Bare and "Ruby, Don't Take Your Love to Town" for Kenny Rogers and First Edition. His big breakthrough, though, didn't come until he revealed what has since become his trademark — the stutter he's had since a bout with malaria at the age of three.

Now, he's recognized not only as a gifted singer and songwriter, but also as a distinctive comic star of TV and the movies. He's well-known for his stories and he's got a good one about a dinner he once had. "I had the privilege of dining at the White House with President and Mrs. Carter. What I remember most was that at the time, I was dipping snuff, and I had no place to spit. So, I tried to use one of the plants for a spittoon. My wife almost died!"

Mel Tillis

Tanya Tucker has grown up in the spotlight. She had her first Top Ten hit at the age of 13 with "Delta Dawn." Since then, she's scored big with such songs as "Blood Red and Goin' Down" and "Would You Lay with Me (in a Field of Stone)," and has averaged about 200 tour dates a year.

One wouldn't expect that she's had much opportunity to become the domestic sort, or given her sassy stage persona, that she'd even want to. But Tanya is quite at home in the kitchen, thank you. "I love to cook for my family," she says, "and for men — especially ones with good appetites. I enjoy trying new recipes on my daddy. He loves for me to cook sirloin steak in the Japanese hibachi style." Tanya admits that she's had some good teachers in the kitchen. "My mother is the greatest cook in the world," she says. "Next to her, I would say that I love to watch the Galloping Gourmet on TV. Whether he knows it or not, we run around our separate kitchens together quite a bit."

Family means a great deal to Tanya. For much of her early career, she toured with her whole family. Today, she's too busy for her family to keep up with. In addition to recording sessions and concert appearances, she's also acted in TV movies and series. So Tanya appreciates times when she can settle down with her family and enjoy a bite to eat. "Thanksgiving is my favorite meal," she says. "It's the one time of the year that my family and I look forward to sitting down and enjoying our turkey together. We go all out on those trimmings, too."

During the rest of the year, Tanya says her favorites from the kitchen are chicken-fried steak ("I love to use tenderized tenderloin, very lean"), taters and gravy. But she isn't picky. "My taste in food," the country rocker explains, "is just like my taste in music — versatile."

What's been her most memorable meal? "It was in Osaka, Japan," she recalls. "I shared a meal with my parents and some Japanese friends while I was on tour there. Our appetizer was shrimp cooked on a hibachi grill. They were presented to me for approval — *live* — and tossed onto the sizzling grill, screaming. Needless to say, so was I! I loved the Kobe beef with the huge garlic pods, but I didn't touch the shrimp." Then there was the dinner she had with her idol, Elvis Presley. "I wanted to be just like him," she confides. "I grew up with him in my heart."

Although Tanya's certainly had her share of memorable, one-of-a-kind meals, she's also used to the very unspectacular food on the road. But she makes it into a kind of adventure. "I check out all the fine restaurants that time and opportunity permit," she says. "I always investigate the house specials. When we're not dining out, we snack on corn chips and home-made guacamole on the bus, or bacon, lettuce and tomato sandwiches on whole wheat toast with a slice of fresh onion on the side. I usually follow that with crispy french fries at 4 am. It's a truckstop delight!" Of course, when she makes that kind of pitstop, so is Tanya.

Tanya Tucker

Conway Twitty has two favorite cooks — his mother, Velma Jenkins, and his wife, Mickey. Conway's favorite dish from Mamaw Jenkins is her white beans — soaked, simmered and seasoned with crumbled meat, salt and pepper. "Conway loves white beans better than anything in the the world," says his mother, "that and meatloaf." If Conway isn't in the mood for white beans or meatloaf, he's probably ready for Mickey's teriyaki steak with bacon-fried rice. "This dish has become so popular around our house that if I'm asked to prepare Conway's favorite dish, this is it," says Mickey, who has been with Conway long enough to know. They were married in 1957.

Mickey found very early in their marriage that Conway likes fresh fish, too. "Early one morning," she recalls, "when we were first married, I got up and discovered fish swimming around in my bathtub. I quickly learned that Conway had gone fishing in the night and had brought home the day's dinner. After figuring out what to do with the fish, I learned to make hushpuppies.

"Conway loves many kinds of foods," she adds, "especially those made with mushrooms, coconut or cooked bananas." One of Mickey's specialties is crunchy baked bananas. Conway also likes cornbread, turnip greens, cabbage, potatoes, pizza and Twittyburgers. "The Twittyburger," Conway explains, "is my version of the hamburger with a slice of batter-fried pineapple. I got the idea for the pineapple while I was on tour in Hawaii in 1959. It really tops off a hamburger."

Conway was born in Friar's Point, Mississippi, with the name of Harold Lloyd Jenkins, after the famous silent film comic. His father ran a ferry boat on the Mississippi River. It was out on the river, traveling between Mississippi and Arkansas, that young Harold started picking guitar. He enjoyed it, almost as much as baseball. In fact, for a while, it was a toss-up between baseball and music for his career because he was good enough for the Philadelphia Phillies to offer him a contract. But when he got out of the Army in 1956 and heard Elvis Presley's "Mystery Train" for the first time, he decided on music and took a new name — from a combination of Conway, Arkansas, and Twitty, Texas. In 1958, he wrote his biggest seller, "It's Only Make Believe," which became a #1 hit in 22 countries. Although he started out as a rockabilly singer like Elvis, in 1965 Conway went country and never looked back. In the summer of 1985, he had his fiftieth #1 hit, "Don't Call Him a Cowboy" — an unprecedented feat for an artist in any genre.

Today, Conway lives at Twitty City, his nine-acre entertainment complex, located just outside of Nashville. Opened in May 1982, the attraction includes Conway's 22 bedroom home, the homes of his four children and Mamaw Jenkins, his own museum, shops and music pavillions. "When I leave my home in the morning to go to the office about 150 yards away," Conway says, "it takes me about an hour just to get there because I stop along the way to talk to visitors." He doesn't mind the delay in the least. "I feel it's something I owe to the fans," he says.

Recipes are, of course, a different matter. But even if he doesn't feel he owes the fans Mickey's cooking secrets, Conway's glad to share a few anyway.

Conway Twitty

Kitty Wells, in her 60s, still plays 165 dates a year and enjoys it. But, she says, "I'm happiest when I can be in my kitchen. To me, the most fun in the world is to work for my family. I love to experiment with new and old recipes. Sometimes I am never satisfied."

Over the years, Kitty has accumulated a lot of tasty recipes, so many in fact that she once published a two-volume cookbook of her favorites. She learned her way around a kitchen from her mother, Kitty's favorite cook. Kitty still remembers when her mother helped her at age seven to bake a cake for the first time for her daddy. Their family meals were traditional back then, and Kitty's still are. Her favorite recipes call for chicken, fish and vegetables. Her favorite holiday meal is Christmas, when she can prepare "turkey, ham and all the fixings."

Kitty was born and reared in Nashville. As a teenager in Nashville in 1936, performing on the WSIX "Dixie Early Birds Show," she met her husband-to-be, Johnny Wright, of the singing team Johnny and Jack. After she and Johnny married in 1937, Kitty became a permanent member of Johnny and Jack's act.

In 1952, Kitty became a solo star in her own right when she recorded "It Wasn't God Who Made Honky Tonk Angels," an answer disc to Hank Thompson's "Wild Side of Life." The #1 hit earned her a place on the Grand Ole Opry, where she remained for the next 15 years. During that period she had 22 more #1 songs, including "Amigo's Guitar" and "One by One," her duet with Red Foley that stayed at the top of the charts for 26 weeks. Each year from 1954 to 1965, *Billboard* magazine voted Kitty #1 Country Music Female Artist. It's with good reason, then, that she's known as the Queen of Country Music.

After nearly 50 years of performing on the road, Kitty has found that her favorite food away from home is chicken and vegetables, Mexican food or Italian dishes. At home in Nashville, when she's not cooking for herself, she likes to eat at Morrison's Cafeteria or the Hermitage House. And of all the meals she's shared with famous people, two meals with former president Richard Nixon stand out in her memory as special occasions: a buffet dinner in San Clemente and "a prayer breakfast with the President, senators, and music industry personalities."

Kitty says she included her recipe for angel biscuits because "it's a favorite with my many fans and friends." As for the orange coconut cake, she says, "It's been in my family for generations. My mother taught me how to make this cake when I was very young. It became my husband's favorite after we were married, and I really enjoyed making it for him."

Kitty Wells

Sharon White probably speaks for her singing partners, father Buck White and sister Cheryl, when she says her favorite cook is her mother, Pat. "No question about it!" says Sharon. She has no question about her mother's best meal either: pot roast with mashed potatoes and carrots, green beans, salad and iced tea.

Sharon's a pretty good cook herself, as husband Ricky Skaggs could tell you. She likes to cook, she says, "when it's not 'have to' and when I have the time — and when *he's* home."

Growing up near Fort Smith, Arkansas, where Buck worked as a pipefitter, Sharon and Cheryl had plenty of lessons in the kitchen with their mother. "Every day Cheryl and I helped Mama prepare dinner when Daddy came home from work," Sharon remembers. "Mother made meat and gravy; Cheryl made tea and set the table; and I'd make mashed potatoes and salad. It was fun, especially on Sunday after church."

That cooperative family spirit has carried right over into their music. Buck and Pat started out performing with another family under the name of Down Home Folks. As the girls grew older, Pat instructed them in singing and Buck taught them how to play musical instruments. In 1967, the girls joined the act. Five years later, in a serious attempt to become professional musicians, the family moved to Nashville. Although Pat left the group in 1973 to concentrate on business at home, the Whites gradually built up a following. In the '80s, they became bonafide stars with their three-part vocals and modern country blend of traditional country and gospel sounds.

Today the Whites are often busy with recording and touring, so they don't get as many chances to be together at the supper table as they used to. "Our meal time was always a time of sharing the events of the day, as well as our hopes, plans and dreams for the future," says Sharon of the old days. "Now those times are special because it is so rare that we can all be together."

One of Sharon's best memories associated with food was a big family cooking project that had humorous results: "In 1975, Mother, Cheryl and I cooked for the New South, the bluegrass group that then included J.D. Crowe, Ricky Skaggs, Jerry Douglas, Bobby Sloane and Mark O'Connor. We made pinto beans, fried potatoes, boiled cabbage, squash and fried cornbread with sliced tomatoes and sliced cantaloupe. The band played at Nashville's Picking Parlor that night . . . and they were too stuffed to pick!"

Because the Whites are often on the road these days, meals can be hectic for Sharon, especially when she has her young daughter, Molly, to mind. So on tour she usually eats quick, non-fattening meals — salads, soups, BLTs and omelettes. "I'll eat eggs in the morning and at night," she says, "because it's hard to go wrong with a scrambled egg sandwich." And salads are "good with any kind of meal and they keep in the fridge."

As for the jambalaya recipe she included here, Sharon says, "Jambalaya is a favorite of Rick's and mine; it's easy to make with one pot."

The Whites

Hank Williams, Jr.

The only son of country music's first superstar, Hank Williams, Jr. began his musical training the moment he was old enough to hold a guitar. As a result, Hank stayed so busy that family meals were no less hurried as a child than they are for him today.

Nevertheless, when it comes to food, Hank will tell you he loves Italian, especially spaghetti and lasagna. But his favorite meal — now, that's a juicy steak and baked potato. Sometimes, though, it's the conversation that makes the meal as when Hank tells you that his all-time eating experience was a meal he once shared with Waylon Jennings. "We talked about old times," he says.

Old times for Bocephus, as Hank's father called him, began with his first professional appearance when he was eight, roughly five years after his father's death. Six years later, Hank was on the concert trail. At 16, he wrote his first song, "Standing in the Shadows," about being the son of a country music legend.

Hank was an immediate, resounding success as both a singer and a writer. But he didn't really come into his own as a country artist until he recovered from a near fatal, 500-foot fall from a Montana mountain top in 1975. Today, Hank's hard-driving, rocking country sound is distinctive enough to have earned him several writers awards and a host of imitators.

Hank Williams, Jr. is clearly his own man now, and he's known for going his own way. For instance, he prefers to make his home with wife Becky and daughter Hilary in Cullman, Alabama, instead of fashionable Nashville.

Holiday meals with his family are always a welcome break from an energetic professional life that, in 1982, garnered nine Hank Williams, Jr. lps on the country charts simultaneously — a feat unequaled by any other country entertainer. Christmas, especially, is a time of respite for Hank. "Then I can take time off, relax, and enjoy my meal more."

When he has the time, he likes to cook because, he explains, "I like to experiment." If you have the time, try out some of these recipes on all your rowdy friends. "They're some of my favorites," says Hank.

When Tammy Wynette was a little girl, she always looked forward to cooking, but not for the reasons most little girls do. By the age of seven, she had already begun working alongside her relatives in the cotton fields of her grandfather's small farm in Itawamba County, Mississippi. "Hoeing, chopping, picking and hating every minute of it," she says. "I learned to cook as a child to stay out of the cotton fields."

Back then, although the family wasn't well off (her father died when she was eight months old), they managed to eat good meals. "Mostly vegetables," says Tammy. "We grew everything we ate. On Sundays we'd have chicken, sometimes with dumplings." To this day, Tammy still enjoys cooking at home for husband George Richey. "When I eat at home now," she says, "we usually have the same type of food I had growing up."

Just 20 years ago, times were lean for Tammy and her girls. Her first marriage had broken up, and she was raising three daughters in Birmingham on a beautician's salary. Meanwhile, she was singing on a local TV show and making occasional trips to Nashville to audition for record producers.

Just when things looked bleakest, she met producer Billy Sherrill, who noticed the tearful quality in her voice. The records that they made vaulted to the top of the charts so many times that Tammy was dubbed the First Lady of Country Music and named the CMA Female Vocalist of the Year four times (1968-1970, 1972). Until recently, her song "Stand By Your Man" was the biggest-selling single in the history of country music. (It now stands second to Dolly Parton's "9 to 5.")

"The only way success has changed us at all is that we have a bigger house to live in and more food," Tammy once told Veronica Visser of *Interview* magazine, "but less time to stay in that house — and we still like hot dogs. Would you believe that a hot dog is still my favorite food? If I had a choice between a steak and a hot dog, why, I'd take the hot dog." She's also fond of pasta and Mexican food when she goes out to eat.

Despite the hard work, Tammy has many pleasant memories of growing up. She recalls, for instance, coming home from school to the savory aroma of her grandmother's fried apple pies. Though that recipe isn't included here, the ones that are, says Tammy, "are some of my favorite foods that I learned to cook as a child."

Tammy Wynette

Index by Star

A

ALABAMA (Mark Herndon)
Barbeque Magnifiqué 115
Deli Dogs 80
Quick-Fry Chicken And Vegtables 128

ALLEN, Deborah
Asparagus Casserole 62
Chocolate Oatmeal Cookies 183
Flounder 136
Holiday Sweet Potatoes 55
Hot Rum Sauce 188

ANDERSON, Bill
Beef Stew 118
Chicken and Broccoli Casserole 131
Corn Pudding 63
Favorite Fruit Cake 166
Hummingbird Cake 164
Orange Cake 170

B

BARE, Bobby
Chocolate Cream Pie 176
Fruit Salad 37
Oyster Casserole 138
Mexican Fiesta Dip 81
Pasta with Carbonara Sauce 106
Pasta with Garlic and Oil 103
Peanut Brittle 183
Potato and Cheese Soup 26
Wild Rice and Shrimp 139

C

CONLEY, Earl Thomas
Beef Stew 117
Chili 101
Chocolate Fudge 180

CORNELIUS, Helen
Cornbread Dressing 58
Curried Chicken Salad 35
Green Salad with Classic Dressing 29
Homemade Chicken Soup 28
Oatmeal Cookies 184
Rainbow Trout 136
Southern Fried Corn 63
Spicy Rib-Eye Beef 116
Sweet Potato Casserole 55
Sweet Southern Pastry 178
Turnip Greens and Hog Jowl 66

D

DANIELS, Charlie
Great Chocolate Cake 161

DICKENS, Little Jimmy
Beef and Egg Noodles 111
Marinated Chicken Breasts 133
Pigs and Taters 126

G

GREENWOOD, Lee
Broccoli and Rice Casserole 60
Cheddar Meatloaf 115
Four-Layer Dessert 189
Oven Fried Chicken 128
Pumpkin Pie 177
Spaghetti Sauce 104

H

HALL, Tom T.
Guacamole Salad 33
River Road Potatoes 57
Skinny Chili 99
Watermelon Wine 191
Wilted Lettuce Salad 28

HARRIS, Emmylou
Broccoli Nut Casserole 61
Chicken Eleganté 131
Sherried Fruit 185

J

JUDDS, THE
Corn Dogs 125
Kraut Salad 31

K

KING, Pee Wee
Baked German Potato Salad 36
Favorite Chili 98
Party Cheese Ball 81

L

LEE, Brenda
Chinese Pork and Veggies 122
Deep Dish Georgia Peach Pie 174
Dilled Steak Roll-Ups 106
Jambalaya Shrimp 137
Southern Spoon Bread 73
Stuffed Pork Chops 123
Sweet Green Tomato Pickles 77

M

MANDRELL, Barbara
Chinese Pepper Steak 107
Knobby Apple Cake 170
Marinated Bean Salad 32
Peach Shortcake 171
Strawberry Pie 175

McENTIRE, Reba
Broccoli Casserole 61
Mexican Cornbread 74
Poke Salad Delight 34
Strawberry Cobbler 171
Sweet Potato Casserole 54

MILSAP, Ronnie
Moonshine 190
Stir-Fry American Style 62

MURPHEY, Michael Martin
Avocado Party Dip 80
Chili Rellenos Con Queso 67
Potato Salad 35

O

OAK RIDGE BOYS, THE
Baked Acorn Squash 66
Banana Nut Bread 76
Barbecue Chicken a la Coca-Cola 134
Broccoli Salad 31
Dry Beef Pie 110
Eggplant Parmesan 64
German Chocolate Caramel Squares 181
Ground Beef and Bean Casserole 111
Hearts of Mine Salad 30
Homemade Ice Cream 188
Hot Biscuits 69
Lasagna 105
Layered Potato Salad 36
Lemonade Pie 175
Mexican Pizza 103
Mountain Man Wild Rice 60
Old Time Family Corn Casserole 64
Peanut Butter Bars 182
Pretzel Salad 37
Pumpkin Pie 177
Raisin Pecan Cake Topping 158
Scalloped Potatoes 56
Yorkshire Pudding with Beef Consommé 58

P

PARTON, Dolly
Apple Stack Pie 179
Banana Pudding 186
Cole Slaw 34
Corn Pone 73
Cowboy Beans 112

PEARL, Minnie
Chess Cake 158
Chess Pie 173
Rolls 72
Spareribs and Sauerkraut 120
Stuffed Pickles 77
Zucchini Squash 65

R

RAVEN, Eddy
Chewy Bread 75
Seafood Gumbo 138

REED, Jerry
Fried Corn 63
Meatloaf 114
Sweet Potato Pie 178

ROGERS, Kenny
Country Chicken Salad 35
Hot Mulled Punch 191

S

SHEPPARD, T. G.
Baked Apricots 185
Cabbage Rolls 109
Cheese Grits 78
Chicken-Shrimp Supreme 139
Coca-Cola Cake 159
Cooked Chicken Sandwiches 130
Praline Crackers 180
Six-Layer Green Salad 29

SKAGGS, Ricky
Chess Pie 173
Fried Cornbread 74
Pinto Beans 68
Sweet Potato Casserole 54

STATLER BROTHERS, THE
Baked Pork Tenderloin and Gravy 121
Bar-B-Que Flatjacks 115
Barbecued Beef 116
Barbecued Chicken 134
Barbecue Sauce 117
Boxley Style Chicken 129
Carrot Cake 167
Cheese Ball 81
Chili 100
Chocolate-Peanut Butter Balls 182
Custard 187
Diet Vegetable Soup 27
Easy Apple Crumb Pie 179
Easy French Bread 71
Green Rice 59
Impossible Cheeseburger Pie 113
Impossible Reuben Pie 119
Meringue-Topped Strawberry Shortcake 172
Mountain Pound Cake 160
Poppy Seed Chicken 132
Sausage 'N' Cheese Brunch Treats 79

STEVENS, Ray
Green Goddess Dip 80
Mexican Casserole 100
"Mr. Mone's" Bean Casserole 68
Raymone's Beanie Weenies 125
Raymone's Beer Biscuits 68
Raymone's Salad 30

STRAIT, George
Carne Guisada 101
Flour Tortillas 75
King Ranch Chicken 130
Spanish Rice 60

T

THOMAS, B. J.
Crock Pot Macaroni and Cheese 56
Fettucine Alfredo 104
French Fries 57
Fudge Brownies 181
Veal Scallopini 124

TILLIS, Mel
Corned Beef and Cabbage 110

Pumpkin Cheesecake 168
Hamburger Stew 118

TUCKER, Tanya
Braided Bread 70
Cheese and Potato Soup 26
Chicken Chili 99
Chicken Fried Steak 119
Chicken Tamales 127
Five-Minute Orange Hash Dessert 190
Fried Green "Tomaters" 66
Guacamole Salad 33
Italian Cream Cake 165
Stroganoff in a Flash 113

TWITTY, Conway
Baked Ham with Peach Honey Glaze 120
Crunchy Baked Bananas 186
Dude's Cornbread 72
Hush Puppies 75
Marinated Barbecued Chicken 134
Mississippi Mud Cake 163
Original Skillet-Fried Potatoes and Okra 56
Teriyaki Steak with Bacon-Fried Rice 108
Texas Fried Chicken 129
Three-Bean Salad 32
Twitty-Burgers 114

W

WELLS, Kitty
Angel Biscuits 69
Chicken and Dumplings 132

Chicken Sauté Continental 127
Orange Coconut Cake 169
7-Up Pound Cake 161

WHITES, The
Apple Butter 76
Chicken Pot Pie 133
Chocolate Cake 162
One Pot Jambalaya 126
Pecan Pie 174
Sauerkraut Salad 31
Slaw 33
Slumgulion Casserole 112
Texas Chili 98
Texas-Style Enchiladas 102

WILLIAMS, Hank, Jr.
Bar-B-Q Deer Cubes 135
Cajun Rice Casserole 59
Country-Style Vegetable and Beef Soup 27
Sausage Treats 79

WYNETTE, Tammy
Banana Pudding 187
Creamed Tuna 135
Eggplant A La Tammy 65
Garlic Cheese Grits 78
Sour Cream Pound Cake 160
Southern Stuffed Bell Peppers 121

Index by Recipe

A

APPETIZERS
Alabama's Deli Dogs 80
Brenda Lee's Dilled Steak Roll-Ups 106
Hank Williams, Jr.'s Sausage Treats 79
The Statler Brothers' Sausage 'N'
    Cheese Brunch Treats 79
Minnie Pearl's Stuffed Pickles 77
Brenda Lee's Sweet Green Tomato Pickles 77
The Statler Brothers' Cheese Ball 81
Pee Wee King's Party Cheese Ball 81

APPLES
Brenda Lee's Stuffed Pork Chops 123
The Oak Ridge Boys' Baked Acorn Squash 66
The Whites' Apple Butter 76
Barbara Mandrell's Knobby Apple Cake 170
The Statler Brothers' Easy Apple Crumb Pie .. 179
Dolly Parton's Apple Stack Pie 179
Ronnie Milsap's Moonshine 190

APRICOTS
Bill Anderson's Orange Cake 170
T.G. Sheppard's Baked Apricots 185

ARTICHOKES
Raymone's Salad 30
The Oak Ridge Boys' Hearts of Mine Salad 30

ASPARAGUS
Raymone's Salad 30
Deborah Allen's Asparagus Casserole 62

AVOCADOS
Tom T. Hall's Guacamole Salad 33
Tanya Tucker's Guacamole Salad 33
Michael Martin Murphey's Avocado
    Party Dip 80
Bobby Bare's Mexican Fiesta Dip 81

B

BACON
Tom T. Hall's Wilted Lettuce Salad 28
The Statler Brothers' Boxley Style Chicken 129
Helen Cornelius' Rainbow Trout 136
Hank Williams, Jr.'s Cajun Rice Casserole 59

BANANAS
The Oak Ridge Boys' Banana Nut Bread 76
Bill Anderson's Hummingbird Cake 164
Conway Twitty's Crunchy Baked Bananas 186
Tammy Wynette's Banana Pudding 187
Dolly Parton's Banana Pudding 186

BEANS
Conway Twitty's Three-Bean Salad 32
Barbara Mandrell's Marinated Bean Salad 32
Dolly Parton's Cowboy Beans 112
The Oak Ridge Boys Ground Beef and
    Bean Casserole 111
Raymone's Beanie Weenies 125
Ricky Skaggs' Pinto Beans 68
"Mr. Mone's" Bean Casserole 68

BEEF
Hank Williams, Jr.'s Country-Style Vegetable
    and Beef Soup 27
The Whites' Texas Chili 98
The Oak Ridge Boys' Dry Beef Pie 110
Mel Tillis' Corned Beef and Cabbage 110
Little Jimmy Dickens' Beef and Egg Noodles .. 111
Earl Thomas Conley's Beef Stew 117
Bill Anderson's Beef Stew 118
The Statler Brothers' Barbecued Beef 116
Helen Cornelius' Spicy Rib-Eye Beef 116
Tanya Tucker's Chicken-Fried Steak 119
Lee Greenwood's Spaghetti Sauce 104
The Statler Brothers' Impossible Reuben Pie . 119
Hank Williams, Jr.'s Bar-B-Q Deer Cubes 135
The Statler Brothers' Boxley Style Chicken 129

BEEF, GROUND

Hank Williams, Jr.'s Country-Style Vegetable
and Beef Soup 27
Reba McEntire's Poke Salad Delight 34
The Statler Brothers' Chili 100
Earl Thomas Conley's Chili 101
Tom T. Hall's Skinny Chili 99
Pee Wee King's Favorite Chili 98
The Whites' Texas-Style Enchiladas 102
The Oak Ridge Boys' Mexican Pizza 103
Raymone's Beanie Weenies 125
Reba McEntire's Mexican Cornbread 74
Conway Twitty's Twitty-Burgers 114
Lee Greenwood's Cheddar Meatloaf 115
Jerry Reed's Meat Loaf 114
The Statler Brothers' Bar-B-Que Flatjacks 115
Mel Tillis' Hamburger Stew 118
The Oak Ridge Boys' Lasagna 105
Ray Stevens' Mexican Casserole 100
Dolly Parton's Cowboy Beans 112
T. G. Sheppard's Cabbage Rolls 109
The Oak Ridge Boys' Ground Beef
and Bean Casserole 111
The Whites' Slumgulion Casserole 112
The Statler Brothers' Impossible
Cheeseburger Pie 113
Tanya Tucker's Stroganoff in a Flash 113

BEEF — STEAK

Brenda Lee's Dilled Steak Roll-Ups 106
Barbara Mandrell's Chinese Pepper Steak 107
Conway Twitty's Teriyaki Steak with
Bacon-Fried Rice 108
George Strait's Carne Guisada 101

BEVERAGES

Tom T. Hall's Watermelon Wine 191
Ronnie Milsap's Moonshine 190
Kenny Rogers' Hot Mulled Punch 191

BREADS, ROLLS, ETC.

Helen Cornelius' Cornbread Dressing 58
The Oak Ridge Boys' Hot Biscuits 69
Kitty Wells' Angel Biscuits 69
Raymone's Beer Biscuits 68
Minnie Pearl's Rolls 72
Brenda Lee's Southern Spoon Bread 73
Tanya Tucker's Braided Bread 70
The Statler Brothers' Easy French Bread 71
Dolly Parton's Corn Pone 73
Conway Twitty's "Dude's Cornbread" 72
Ricky Skaggs' Fried Cornbread 74
Reba McEntire's Mexican Cornbread 74
The Oak Ridge Boys' Banana Nut Bread 76
Eddy Raven's Chewy Bread 75
Conway Twitty's Hush Puppies 75
George Strait's Flour Tortillas 75

BROCCOLI

The Oak Ridge Boys' Broccoli Salad 31
Emmylou Harris' Chicken Eleganté 131
Bill Anderson's Chicken and
Broccoli Casserole 131
The Statler Brothers' Green Rice 59
Lee Greenwood's Broccoli and Rice Casserole ... 60
Emmylou Harris' Broccoli Nut Casserole 61
Reba McEntire's Broccoli Casserole 61

BRUSSEL SPROUTS

The Oak Ridge Boys' Hearts of Mine Salad 30

C

CABBAGE

The Whites' Sauerkraut Salad 31
The Judds' Kraut Salad 31
Dolly Parton's Cole Slaw 34
The Whites' Slaw 33
The Oak Ridge Boy's Layered Potato Salad 36

T. G. Sheppard's Cabbage Rolls 109
Mel Tillis' Corned Beef and Cabbage 110
The Statler Brothers' Impossible Reuben Pie .. 119
Minnie Pearl's Spareribs and Sauerkraut 120

CAKES

Minnie Pearl's Chess Cake 158
T. G. Sheppard's Coca-Cola Cake 159
The Statler Brothers' Mountain Pound Cake .. 160
Tammy Wynette's Sour Cream Pound Cake 160
Kitty Wells' 7-Up Pound Cake 161
Conway Twitty's Mississippi Mud Cake 163
Charlie Daniels' Great Chocolate Cake 161
The Whites' Chocolate Cake 162
Bill Anderson's Hummingbird Cake 164
Tanya Tucker's Italian Cream Cake 165
Bill Anderson's Favorite Fruit Cake 166
The Statler Brothers' Carrot Cake 167
Mel Tillis' Pumpkin Cheesecake 168
Kitty Wells' Orange Coconut Cake 169
Bill Anderson's Orange Cake 170
Barbara Mandrell's Knobby Apple Cake 170
Barbara Mandrell's Peach Shortcake 171
The Statler Brothers' Meringue-Topped
    Strawberry-Shortcake 172
Reba McEntire's Strawberry Cobbler 171

CANDY

Earl Thomas Conley's Chocolate Fudge 180
The Statler Brothers' Chocolate-Peanut
    Butter Balls 182
Bobby Bare's Peanut Brittle 183

CARROTS

The Statler Brothers' Carrot Cake 167
Ronnie Milsap's Moonshine 190

CHEESE

Tanya Tucker's Cheese and Potato Soup 26
Bobby Bare's Potato and Cheese Soup 26
T.G. Sheppard's Six Layer Green Salad 29
Raymone's Salad 30
Lee Greenwood's Cheddar Meatloaf 115
The Oak Ridge Boys' Lasagna 105
The Whites' Texas-Style Enchiladas 102
The Oak Ridge Boys' Mexican Pizza 103

The Statler Brothers' Impossible Reuben Pie . 119
Emmylou Harris' Chicken Eleganté 131
Tanya Tucker's Chicken Tamales 127
T.G. Sheppard's Chicken-Shrimp Supreme 139
Bobby Bare's Wild Rice and Shrimp 139
B.J. Thomas' Crock Pot Macaroni and Cheese .. 56
The Statler Brothers' Green Rice Pie 59
Lee Greenwood's Broccoli and Rice Casserole ... 60
Reba McEntire's Broccoli Casserole 61
Deborah Allen's Asparagus Casserole 62
The Oak Ridge Boys' Eggplant Parmesan 64
Michael Martin Murphey's Chili Rellenos
    Con Queso 67
T.G. Sheppard's Cheese Grits 78
Tammy Wynette's Garlic Cheese Grits 78
Hank Williams, Jr.'s Sausage Treats 79
The Statler Brothers' Sausage 'N'
    Cheese Brunch Treats 79
Alabama's Deli Dogs 80
Minnie Pearl's Stuffed Pickles 77
Bobby Bare's Mexican Fiesta Dip 81
The Statler Brothers' Cheese Ball 81
Pee Wee King's Party Cheese Ball 81
Mel Tillis' Pumpkin Cheesecake 168

CHICKEN

Helen Cornelius' Homemade Chicken Soup 28
Helen Cornelius' Curried Chicken Salad 35
Kenny Rogers' Country Chicken Salad 35
Tanya Tucker's Chicken Chili 99
The Whites' "One Pot" Jambalaya 126
Lee Greenwood's Oven Fried Chicken 128
Conway Twitty's Texas Fried Chicken 129
Emmylou Harris' Chicken Eleganté 131
The Statler Brothers' Boxley Style Chicken 129
George Strait's King Ranch Chicken 130
Bill Anderson's Chicken and
    Broccoli Casserole 131
Alabama's Quick-Fry Chicken
    and Vegetables 128
The Whites' Chicken Pot Pie 133
Kitty Wells' Chicken and Dumplings 132
The Statler Brothers' Poppy Seed Chicken 132
Little Jimmy Dickens' Marinated
    Chicken Breasts 133

The Oak Ridge Boys' Barbecue Chicken
    a la Coca-Cola 134
Conway Twitty's Marinated Barbecued Chicken . 134
The Statler Brothers' Barbecued Chicken 134
Tanya Tucker's Chicken Tamales 127
Kitty Wells' Chicken Sauté Continental 127
T.G. Sheppard's Cooked Chicken Sandwiches .. 130
T.G. Sheppard's Chicken-Shrimp Supreme 139

CHILI
The Statler Brothers' Chili 100
Earl Thomas Conley's Chili 101
Tom T. Hall's Skinny Chili 99
The Whites' Texas Chili 98
Pee Wee King's Favorite Chili 98
Tanya Tucker's Chicken Chili 99

CHOCOLATE
T.G. Sheppard's Coca-Cola Cake 159
Conway Twitty's Mississippi Mud Cake 163
Charlie Daniels' Great Chocolate Cake 161
The Whites' Chocolate Cake 162
Bobby Bare's Chocolate Cream Pie 176
B.J. Thomas' Fudge Brownies 181
The Oak Ridge Boys' Peanut Butter Bars 182
The Oak Ridge Boys' German Chocolate
    Caramel Squares 181
Deborah Allen's Chocolate Oatmeal Cookies 183
Lee Greenwood's Four-Layer Dessert 189
Earl Thomas Conley's Chocolate Fudge 180
The Statler Brothers' Chocolate-Peanut
    Butter Balls 182

COOKIE VARIETIES
T.G. Sheppard's Praline Crackers 180
B.J. Thomas' Fudge Brownies 181
The Oak Ridge Boys' Peanut Butter Bars 182
The Oak Ridge Boys' German Chocolate
    Caramel Squares 181
Deborah Allen's Chocolate Oatmeal Cookies 183
Helen Cornelius' Oatmeal Cookies 184

CORN
The Whites' Slumgulion Casserole 112
Tammy Wynette's Southern Stuffed
    Bell Peppers 121

Helen Cornelius' Southern-Fried Corn 63
Jerry Reed's Fried Corn 63
Bill Anderson's Corn Pudding 63
The Oak Ridge Boys' Old Time Family
    Corn Casserole 64
Reba McEntire's Mexican Cornbread 74

CUSTARD
The Statler Brothers' Custard 187

D

DIPS
Tom T. Hall's Guacamole Salad 33
Tanya Tucker's Guacamole Salad 33
Michael Martin Murphey's Avocado
    Party Dip 80
Bobby Bare's Mexican Fiesta Dip 81
Ray Stevens' Green Goddess Dip 80

F

FRUIT
Bobby Bare's Fruit Salad 37
The Oak Ridge Boys' Pretzel Salad 37
Conway Twitty's Baked Ham
    with Peach Honey Glaze 120
Bill Anderson's Favorite Fruit Cake 166
Emmylou Harris' Sherried Fruit 185
Tom T. Hall's Watermelon Wine 191

H

HAM
Tammy Wynette's Southern Stuffed
    Bell Peppers 121
Conway Twitty's Baked Ham
    with Peach Honey Glaze 120
Brenda Lee's Jambalaya Shrimp 137

I

ICE CREAM
The Oak Ridge Boys' Homemade Ice Cream .. 188

ICINGS & TOPPINGS
The Oak Ridge Boys' Raisin Pecan
    Cake Topping (See CAKES) 158

M

MEXICAN

Ray Stevens' Mexican Casserole 100
The Whites' Texas-Style Enchiladas 102
The Oak Ridge Boys' Mexican Pizza 103
George Strait's Carne Guisada 101
George Strait's King Ranch Chicken 130
Tanya Tucker's Chicken Tamales 127
George Strait's Spanish Rice 60
Michael Martin Murphey's Chili Rellenos
    Con Queso 67
Reba McEntire's Mexican Cornbread 74
George Strait's Flour Tortillas 75
Tom T. Hall's Guacamole Salad 33
Tanya Tucker's Guacamole Salad 33
Michael Martin Murphey's Avocado
    Party Dip 80
Bobby Bare's Mexican Fiesta Dip 81

N

NUTS

Emmylou Harris' Broccoli Nut Casserole 61
The Oak Ridge Boys' Banana Nut Bread 76
Bill Anderson's Hummingbird Cake 164
Bill Anderson's Favorite Fruit Cake 166
The Whites' Pecan Pie 174
T.G. Sheppard's Praline Crackers 180
Bobby Bare's Peanut Brittle 183

O

OKRA

Conway Twitty's Original Skillet-Fried
    Potatoes and Okra 56
Hank Williams, Jr.'s Cajun Rice Casserole 59

ORANGES

Kitty Wells' Orange Coconut Cake 169
Tanya Tucker's Five-Minute Orange
    Hash Dessert 190

P

PASTA

Pee Wee King's Favorite Chili 98
Little Jimmy Dickens' Beef and Egg Noodles .. 111

The Oak Ridge Boys' Ground Beef and
    Bean Casserole 111
The Whites' Slumgulion Casserole 112
Tanya Tucker's Stroganoff in a Flash 113
B.J. Thomas' Fettucine Alfredo 104
The Oak Ridge Boys' Lasagna 105
Bobby Bare's Pasta with Carbonara Sauce 106
Bobby Bare's Pasta with Garlic and Oil 103
B.J. Thomas' Veal Scallopini 124
B.J. Thomas' Crock Pot Macaroni
    and Cheese 56

PEACHES

Barbara Mandrell's Peach Shortcake 171
Brenda Lee's Deep Dish Georgia Peach Pie 174

PEAS

T.G. Sheppard's Six Layer Green Salad 29
Barbara Mandrell's Marinated Bean Salad 32
Tammy Wynette's Southern
    Stuffed Bell Peppers 121
Tammy Wynette's Creamed Tuna 135

PEPPERS

Tammy Wynette's Southern Stuffed
    Bell Peppers 121
The Oak Ridge Boys' Mountain
    Man Wild Rice 60

PIES

Ricky Skaggs' Chess Pie 173
The Whites' Pecan Pie 174
Brenda Lee's Deep Dish Georgia Peach Pie 174
The Statler Brothers' Easy Apple Crumb Pie .. 179
Dolly Parton's Apple Stack Pie 179
Barbara Mandrell's Strawberry Pie 175
The Oak Ridge Boys' Pumpkin Pie 177
The Oak Ridge Boys' Dry Beef Pie 110
The Statler Brothers' Impossible
    Cheeseburger Pie 113
The Statler Brothers' Impossible
    Reuben Pie 119
The Whites' Chicken Pot Pie 133
Helen Cornelius' Sweet Southern Pastry 178
Minnie Pearl's Chess Pie 173
Lee Greenwood's Pumpkin Pie 177
Bobby Bare's Chocolate Cream Pie 176

The Oak Ridge Boys' Lemonade Pie 175
Jerry Reed's Sweet Potato Pie 178

PINEAPPLES
Conway Twitty's Twitty-Burgers 114
Conway Twitty's Texas Fried Chicken 129
Little Jimmy Dicken's Marinated Chicken
    Breasts 133
Conway Twitty's Marinated Barbecued
    Chicken 134
Bill Anderson's Hummingbird Cake 164

PORK – SAUSAGE, ETC.
T.G. Sheppard's Cabbage Rolls 109
The Statler Brothers' Baked Pork
    Tenderloin and Gravy 121
Minnie Pearl's Spareribs and Sauerkraut 120
Brenda Lee's Chinese Pork and Veggies 122
Brenda Lee's Stuffed Pork Chops 123
Raymone's Beanie Weenies 125
The Judds' Corn Dogs 125
Little Jimmy Dickens' Pigs and Taters 126
The Whites' "One Pot" Jambalaya 126
Hank Williams, Jr.'s Sausage Treats 79
The Statler Brothers' Sausage 'N'
    Cheese Brunch Treats 79
Alabama's Deli Dogs 80

POTATOES
Tanya Tucker's Cheese and Potato Soup 26
Bobby Bare's Potato and Cheese Soup 26
The Oak Ridge Boys' Layered Potato Salad 36
Michael Martin Murphey's Potato Salad 35
Pee Wee King's Baked German Potato Salad 36
The Oak Ridge Boys' Dry Beef Pie 110
Little Jimmy Dickens' Pigs and Taters 126
Ricky Skaggs' Sweet Potato Casserole 54
Reba McEntire's Favorite Sweet
    Potato Casserole 54
Helen Cornelius' Sweet Potato Casserole 55
Deborah Allen's Holiday Sweet Potatoes 55
Tom T. Hall's River Road Potatoes 57
B.J. Thomas' French Fries 57
Conway Twitty's Original Skillet-Fried
    Potatoes and Okra 56
The Oak Ridge Boys' Scalloped Potatoes 56
Jerry Reed's Sweet Potato Pie 178

PUDDING
Tammy Wynette's Banana Pudding 187
Dolly Parton's Banana Pudding 186
Lee Greenwood's Four-Layer Dessert 189

PUMPKIN
Mel Tillis' Pumpkin Cheesecake 168
The Oak Ridge Boys' Pumpkin Pie 177
Lee Greenwood's Pumpkin Pie 177

R

RICE
The Oak Ridge Boys' Mountain Man
    Wild Rice 60
George Strait's Spanish Rice 60
Hank Williams, Jr.'s Cajun Rice Casserole 59
The Statler Brothers' Green Rice 59
Lee Greenwood's Broccoli and Rice Casserole ... 60
Reba McEntire's Broccoli Casserole 61
Conway Twitty's Teriyaki Steak
    with Bacon-Fried Rice 108
T.G. Sheppard's Cabbage Rolls 109
Jerry Reed's Meatloaf 114
The Whites' "One Pot" Jambalaya 126
T.G. Sheppard's Chicken-Shrimp Supreme 139
Brenda Lee's Jambalaya Shrimp 137
Bobby Bare's Wild Rice and Shrimp 139
Eddy Raven's Seafood Gumbo 138

S

SALADS
T.G. Sheppard's Six Layer Green Salad 29
Tom T. Hall's Wilted Lettuce Salad 28
Raymone's Salad 30
Helen Cornelius' Green Salad with
    Classic Dressing 29
The Oak Ridge Boys' Hearts of Mine Salad 30
Reba McEntire's Poke Salad Delight 34
Conway Twitty's Three-Bean Salad 32
Barbara Mandrell's Marinated Bean Salad 32
The Oak Ridge Boys' Broccoli Salad 31
The Whites' Sauerkraut Salad 31
The Judds' Kraut Salad 31
Dolly Parton's Cole Slaw 34
The Whites' Slaw 33
Tom T. Hall's Guacamole Salad 33

Tanya Tucker's Guacamole Salad 33
The Oak Ridge Boys' Layered Potato Salad 36
Michael Martin Murphey's Potato Salad 35
Pee Wee King's Baked German Potato Salad 36
Helen Cornelius' Curried Chicken Salad 35
Kenny Rogers' Country Chicken Salad 35
Bobby Bare's Fruit Salad 37
The Oak Ridge Boys' Pretzel Salad 37

SAUCES
Lee Greenwood's Spaghetti Sauce 104
Conway Twitty's Baked Ham with
    Peach Honey Glaze 120
The Oak Ridge Boys' Barbecue Chicken
    a la Coca-Cola 134
Conway Twitty's Marinated
    Barbequed Chicken 134
The Statler Brothers' Barbeque Sauce 117
Alabama's Barbeque Magnifiqué 115
Deborah Allen's Hot Rum Sauce 188

SEAFOOD
T.G. Sheppard's Chicken-Shrimp Supreme 139
Helen Cornelius' Rainbow Trout 136
Deborah Allen's Flounder 136
Bobby Bare's Oyster Casserole 138
Brenda Lee's Jambalaya Shrimp 137
Bobby Bare's Wild Rice and Shrimp 139
Eddy Raven's Seafood Gumbo 138
Tammy Wynette's Creamed Tuna 135

SOUPS
Tanya Tucker's Cheese and Potato Soup 26
Bobby Bare's Potato and Cheese Soup 26
The Statler Brothers' Diet Vegetable Soup 27
Hank Williams, Jr.'s Country-Style Vegetable
    and Beef Soup 27
Helen Cornelius' Homemade Chicken Soup 28

SQUASH
Tammy Wynette's Eggplant a la Tammy 65
The Oak Ridge Boys' Eggplant Parmesan 64
Minnie Pearl's Zucchini Squash 65
The Oak Ridge Boys' Baked Acorn Squash 66

STEWS
Mel Tillis' Hamburger Stew 118
Earl Thomas Conley's Beef Stew 117
Bill Anderson's Beef Stew 118

STRAWBERRIES
The Statler Brothers' Meringue-Topped
    Strawberry Shortcake 172
Reba McEntire's Strawberry Cobbler 171
Barbara Mandrell's Strawberry Pie 175

T

TOMATOES
Ray Stevens' Mexican Casserole 100
The Oak Ridge Boys' Mexican Pizza 103
George Strait's Carne Guisada 101
Tammy Wynette's Southern
    Stuffed Bell Peppers 121
George Strait's King Ranch Chicken 130
Kitty Wells' Chicken Sauté Continental 127
Alabama's Quick-Fry Chicken and Vegetables .. 128
Brenda Lee's Jambalaya Shrimp 137
George Strait's Spanish Rice 60
Hank Williams, Jr.'s Cajun Rice Casserole 59
Tammy Wynette's Eggplant a la Tammy 65
Tanya Tucker's Fried Green "Tomaters" 66
Brenda Lee's Sweet Green
    Tomato Pickles 77

TURNIPS
    Helen Cornelius' Turnip Greens
        and Hog Jowl 66

V

VEAL
    B.J. Thomas' Veal Scallopini 124

VEGETABLES
    The Statler Brothers' Diet Vegetable Soup 27
    Hank Williams, Jr.'s Country-Style Vegetable
        and Beef Soup 27
    Raymone's Salad 30
    Helen Cornelius' Green Salad with
        Classic Dressing 29
    The Oak Ridge Boys' Hearts of Mine Salad 30
    Barbara Mandrell's Marinated Bean Salad 32
    The Oak Ridge Boys' Broccoli Salad 31
    Brenda Lee's Dilled Steak Roll-Ups 106
    Barbara Mandrell's Chinese Pepper Steak 107
    Mel Tillis' Hamburger Stew 118
    Earl Thomas Conley's Beef Stew 117
    Bill Anderson's Beef Stew 118
    The Oak Ridge Boys' Mexican Pizza 103
    Tammy Wynette's Southern
        Stuffed Bell Peppers 121
    Brenda Lee's Chinese Pork and Veggies 122
    Alabama's Quick-Fry Chicken and Vegetables .. 128
    The Whites' Chicken Pot Pie 133
    Kitty Wells' Chicken Sauté Continental 127
    The Oak Ridge Boys' "Yorkshire Pudding"
        with Beef Consommé 58
    Helen Cornelius' Cornbread Dressing 58
    Ronnie Milsap's Stir-Fry American Style 62

NOTES:

Cooking with Country Music Stars Cookbook
Order Form

Please send me _____ copies of *Cooking with Country Music Stars* cookbook at $16.95 each.

Subtotal _____
* Shipping and Handling _____
** Sales Tax _____
Total Enclosed _____

* Add $1.50 postage and handling, plus 25 cents for each additional book ordered.
** Jefferson Parish residents add 8% sales tax. All other Louisiana residents add 4% sales tax.

See reverse side for mailing instructions.
Prices subject to change without notice.

Cooking with Country Music Stars Cookbook
Order Form

Please send me _____ copies of *Cooking with Country Music Stars* cookbook at $16.95 each.

Subtotal _____
* Shipping and Handling _____
** Sales Tax _____
Total Enclosed _____

* Add $1.50 postage and handling, plus 25 cents for each additional book ordered.
** Jefferson Parish residents add 8% sales tax. All other Louisiana residents add 4% sales tax.

See reverse side for mailing instructions.
Prices subject to change without notice.

Cooking with Country Music Stars Cookbook
Order Form

Please send me _____ copies of *Cooking with Country Music Stars* cookbook at $16.95 each.

Subtotal _____
* Shipping and Handling _____
** Sales Tax _____
Total Enclosed _____

* Add $1.50 postage and handling, plus 25 cents for each additional book ordered.
** Jefferson Parish residents add 8% sales tax. All other Louisiana residents add 4% sales tax.

See reverse side for mailing instructions.
Prices subject to change without notice.

Mail order to:

Pelican Publishing Company, P.O. Box 189, Gretna, LA 70054

**Enclosed please find my check or money order made out to
Pelican Publishing Company for $_____.
(DO NOT SEND CASH.)**

(Check or money order amount must be same as total on reverse side.)

Send order to:

Name_____

Address_____

City_____State_____Zip_____

Telephone #_____

If you have ordered more than one book to be sent to different addresses, enclose card with additional addresses.

Mail order to:

Pelican Publishing Company, P.O. Box 189, Gretna, LA 70054

**Enclosed please find my check or money order made out to
Pelican Publishing Company for $_____.
(DO NOT SEND CASH.)**

(Check or money order amount must be same as total on reverse side.)

Send order to:

Name_____

Address_____

City_____State_____Zip_____

Telephone #_____

If you have ordered more than one book to be sent to different addresses, enclose card with additional addresses.

Mail order to:

Pelican Publishing Company, P.O. Box 189, Gretna, LA 70054

**Enclosed please find my check or money order made out to
Pelican Publishing Company for $_____.
(DO NOT SEND CASH.)**

(Check or money order amount must be same as total on reverse side.)

Send order to:

Name_____

Address_____

City_____State_____Zip_____

Telephone #_____

If you have ordered more than one book to be sent to different addresses, enclose card with additional addresses.